What others :

How To Be A Christian Boss

"A great blend of balancing one's responsibility as a leader in the business world with the guidance that comes from established biblical principles.... a must read if you own a business or manage people."

Wayne Wallace, LTCP, Agency Field Executive, State Farm Insurance

"I have had the privilege of knowing Richard Nelson for the past several years. During this time I have grown to understand that his life experiences and love for Christ give him much to offer. Richard has been a successful teacher and businessman in the community as well as a trusted elder and brother in the church. I have had the opportunity to sit under his teachings in many different venues including in the meetings of the church, specific instructional classes and individually through lunches and fellowship. His wisdom, coupled with the common sense he offers in *How to be a Christian Boss*, is invaluable whether you desire to be a leader of an existing entity or to be self-employed.

Richard Nelson has assembled a resource that is informative, helpful and practical. I found the book challenging and thought provoking. I encourage you to use this book as a tool to assist you to be a better "boss" as you grow in your pursuit of our Savior."

Brian Sweatt, Administrator, Lighthouse Christian School

"Self-employment "chose me" rather than me choosing it. Being a single mom, caring for a sick child, while needing to still earn a living, left me unable to fit into the confines of a 9 -5 job. So instead I became "self-employed". I quickly discovered I could never competently meet the rigorous demands of planning, scheduling, operating and intelligently growing a small business.

For me, reading this book sparked light, comfort, inspiration and the "Aha!" of realization page after page. I am greatly helped by reading *How To Be A Christian Boss* and, whatever your situation is, you will be, too."

Andrea Benoit, Self-employed Business Owner,
InnerNet Sales Company

"I felt like I was holding a trusted friend with Nelson's *How To Be A Christian Boss.* His wisdom from years of experience is evident from page to page. Greater still is his integration of life in business with life in Jesus Christ. When Christ is experienced there, in the heart, then the experience of Him in business practices will flow and truly be from Him. This just might change your business and your personal life!"

Rev. Dale B. Still, Prison Minister/Counselor
and Small Business Owner

"I have enjoyed reading Richard's books and writings for several years now, but feel *How To Be A Christian Boss* may be his best effort yet. His artistic injection of humor, at just the right moment, will often lighten up some of the more difficult to absorb lessons. Richard has practiced "doing the right thing" for so long that now he is well able to help the rest of us consider doing so (or perhaps 'more so'!) ourselves, both as we examine the life he lives, and gain insight from his teaching and writing."

Curtis Rose, Sculpture Artist, Poet and Author

Living The Legacy

A testimony by Nathan P. Nelson,
Eldest son of Richard A. Nelson,
and Sole Proprietor of NPN Construction Co.
Cane Ridge, TN

"The author of this book is my dad and I am the oldest of four children. You need to read this book- even if you are not in business but just want to live as a Christian in the world in a way that makes sense. These pages are not just instructive. They are a testimony of how important principles and truths have become a way of thinking and a way of living for my dad, my mom and my whole family. As a result of hearing Dad's words and watching him live as he struggled to pay the bills, love his family and serve the Lord in the church all at the same time, through the many years I have learned much and been helped so much.

My brother, Steven, and I are both construction contractors and each own our own business. Our sisters, Robin and Amy, both work for other professionals in the medical field. From the time each of us was two years old, we all began learning to use our own tools and take care of our own things every day.

Steven and I not only began learning how to use our own construction tools before we started first grade, but we also soon learned to sew, cook, do the dishes and care for practical things day by day in our home. Robin and Amy not only learned to care for things that prepared them to be the wonderful wives and mothers they are today in their homes, but they also learned to clean the construction sites with us and with Mom. I still remember photos of the girls using a jackhammer while in elementary school because they wanted to help us boys and Dad remove a concrete driveway.

We not only learned how to work well, but we learned to enjoy working. By the time we discovered work was sometimes really hard, we already had learned to enjoy the importance of it, the value of it and the reward of it. We worked together, prayed together, laughed together, and enjoyed church things together. When our classmates were thinking about getting a summer job in high school for minimum wage, Steven and I were already accomplished journeymen and had our own company installing cabinets in new subdivisions when we were not at school.

Each of us became independent enough to take care of ourselves before we were eighteen years old, yet we always wanted to be together voluntarily as a family. Years later, all four of us got married in the same year, yet Dad and Mom had very little expense or time pressures because each of us had learned to be responsible for our finances, planning and so forth.

Today, Dad and Mom have ten grandchildren and each of them is being trained at home in the same way as we were in responsibility and enjoyment of life. No times are happier than when all of us are together, and we all live within thirty minutes of each other and are together very often. I think we have all learned the value of working for ourselves or for others, but that work is not an end in itself. It is a place where we practice living, but the work is for our family and strengthens our desire to be useful to God.

I've shared these things with you to give you a taste of what you might discover in this book. Yes, it has helpful instruction, but so much more. It is instruction that issues from Dad and Mom's experience of every point on every page. To learn something can be really inspiring, but what Dad wrote here is not just good information. It is the overflow of his life at work which our family has seen and heard and learned to imitate since I was a child. I am thankful to the Lord that my family grew up in this kind of atmosphere, and I am sure you will be inspired and helped by what is presented to you here in Dad's instructive testimony of *How to be a Christian Boss*."

How To Be A Christian Boss:

Guidelines for Believers Considering Self-employment or Business Management

By
Richard A. Nelson

Printed in the United States of America
ISBN 978-0-981851228

Unless otherwise indicated, Scripture quotations are from the King James Version of the Bible.

Cover design and book formatting by Becky Yoder

Morning Star Publishing Co.

© RICHARD A. NELSON
13405 OLD HICKORY BLVD
CANE RIDGE, TN 37013
richard@mstarpublishing.com
www.mstarpublishing.com

Table of Contents

Foreword

The printed words of Richard A. Nelson communicate a heart and brain shaped by years of work in the business world and years of commitment to Jesus Christ. Basic philosophies and practical advice fill the pages of this easily read book. Some readers may find the content challenging, however, since Nelson's suggestions are guided by a call for integrity, honesty, fairness, and ethics in each of life's decisions.

I first met Richard Nelson when he enrolled as a student at Oxford Graduate School in Tennessee. His new academic adventure was an example of the lifelong learning activities he describes in his book as characteristic of a successful individual. The purpose of enrolling in the graduate school was to foster the development of skills which enhance adults' ability to integrate Christian principles and every area of society. This book provides guidance from a contractor, developer, and business owner whose life goal has been to personify that type of integration.

As I read the book, I felt as if I were being mentored by a giant in the field. His practical techniques were easy to understand in terms of both how to implement them and why each is important. Richard's writings are an example of "giving back" to society valuable lessons one has learned through years of experience. His book includes business lessons he taught to his own sons and now shares with all readers, as well. If you are contemplating self-employment or business management, read this book to identify many issues which require consideration as you make that important decision.

From my perspective, a key concept developed throughout the book is the importance of setting and living by priorities. Relationships with God and family are listed before work relationships. Apparent in his words is that this book is written for the every-day-of-the-week Christian whose beliefs and values are the same regardless of location or individuals present. He does not use a preachy style either in print or in practice, but he is a definite example of one who lives Matthew 6:33, "Seek ye first the kingdom of God and His righteousness, and all things shall be added unto you."

In a good book, the writer and book are one – Richard Nelson *is* a Christian Boss!

Rebecca F. Tucker, EdD
President/CEO
Oxford Graduate School
Dayton, TN

Preface

Why do I write this? Over many years, many believers have asked me how to be a Christian and maintain a testimony of Christ while engaged in the business world. This inquiry implies, that for at least some sincere believers, there seems to be a conflict between the two. Yes, there is a huge conflict, in a sense, but in another sense it is not a problem. It depends much on our own experience before God, our understanding of the scriptures and how we perceive our place in the world day by day.

I am hopeful that what I share with you will untangle some of the conflict and fear you may have in this matter. Although I am blessed to have learned much of the Lord and about the world while being in the world of construction and real estate and public school teaching, I have also failed much.

I write with the hope to serve sincere believers in the workplace; but, be warned: sincerity requires much of the one who is sincere. Although we ought to be sincere in all things, we ought not to expect good results merely because of our endeavor to be genuine. It is tempting to assume that we will be honored by God, that we will be blessed merely because we are believers, or that we will be rescued out of a difficulty simply because we believe in Christ and are sincere about our faith.

Such assumption is not scriptural and such assumption is misplaced. God is a Person; sincerity is an attitude. We must trust in God; we must not trust in sincerity in and of itself. Many sincere seekers of the Lord who do not realize this find themselves in disastrous circumstances. *I have trapped myself in serious decisions more than once along the way because I thought my sincerity would rescue me. It did not and it usually will not.*

In fact, the devil and weakness of character often take advantage of one who is sincere. Sometimes I have trusted someone else because he seemed sincere, but I paid a big price. Instead of receiving protection, you may expose yourself to deceit and difficulties. In no place is this lesson more crucial to learn than in the daily business world. Just so you know, this discussion is not a Bible study, per se. It is more a fellowship with you of my personal experience as a Christian in the business world.

While we ought to learn from those who have led us in what we should do, the instruction is often more on what *not* to do. When employing others or supervising others, we should keep this in mind. However, I must confess that even when others have tried to teach me well, my failures have often become more instructive to me than some of the things I have done well.

It seems this is a principle that you also might find helpful. After all, if David had not failed in his life, we would never have had the wisdom of Solomon to teach us so much. We ought not to excuse ourselves, anymore than David excused himself, but let us humbly worship God for whatever "Solomon" may be born from the midst of our conflicts, challenges and failures. In the end, Solomon wins and God is praised!

The subject at hand suggests that there is such a thing as "a Christian boss". In a real sense, there is not. The weight of such a title is heavy and perhaps nearly unachievable. Perhaps we are talking about a boss who is a Christian.

Saying it the latter way brings quite a different view. In our day and time there are many Christians who are "closet believers". No one would ever guess they are believers in the Jesus who lived for God, died for man and rose again to impart such a Life into those who genuinely believe in Him.

So, then, how can we talk about being “a Christian boss”? This discussion is especially for believers who are interested either in self-employment or in a management position with an existing company or profession.

(In fact, the principles we will discuss are valid and pragmatic, whatever the spiritual concept of the person, believer or not. For example, I know of an unbeliever who often read the book of Proverbs so he could learn how to do business right and treat people properly).

I hope and pray this little book will encourage you to have a large heart for God and man, even as you walk daily within your place in the world of work.

The Author

...but let us humbly worship God for whatever "Solomon" may be born from the midst of our conflicts, challenges and failures. In the end, Solomon wins and God is praised!

So, you are a Christian?
What does that have to do with your job?

Introduction:
So, you are a Christian? What does that have to do with your job?

The life of a Christian has a mysterious root. The world of work in the business domain is quite the opposite at its root. The world indeed has its mystery also, but the two mysteries have different sources. A believer is a child of the Real but Unseen, a son of another Father, a citizen of another Kingdom. Meanwhile he needs to engage in a world that is opposed to all that his God is for. He needs to learn to work well and to demonstrate the ultimate practicality of his redeemed, uplifted humanity.

On the one hand, he is a son of earth, and he must work in the economy of the world and provide for his human living and that of his family. On the other hand, he is a son of God, a citizen of a heavenly kingdom with a mysterious, spiritual economy. The challenge to believers is to set the heart and mind on "the things above", even while working "on things below". To be a Christian, truly, is to live by a divine source amid a fallen domain.

To be a "Christian boss" is to function with focused responsibility and expected accountability in an earthly domain.

To be in the business world with responsibility is to function in a world under the relentless influence of an atmosphere that is in total opposition to God. To be a Christian in the business world is to be a person living a dual citizenship. It is to live by Christ as the source of daily living even while in the midst of daily affairs of the world.

To be a Christian, then, is to have a heavenly source. To be a "Christian boss" is to function with focused responsibility and expected accountability in an earthly domain. For the normal believer, it is to be under the laws and government of the same fallen system over whom he is destined to rule in the age to come. It is to appropriately lead others in a maturing, godly humanity, even while yearning for the Lord's kingdom to replace the flawed, deceptive, worldly system in which we live and work.

On the surface, it appears there may be a conflict between being a spiritual person and being involved in the business world. This would imply we need to choose whether to be "spiritual" or "be in the business world". I think it is important to realize this is not an either/or issue, but an issue of learning how to walk with the Lord while we are in our daily life at work. In the light of John 17:15-16, I think we should pray that the Lord will teach us how to become spiritual and how to remain spiritual throughout the day while we are working. It is a natural and utterly unbiblical concept that a believer must escape from contact with the world in order to focus on God.

It is a natural and utterly unbiblical concept that a believer must escape from contact with the world in order to focus on God.

"Going to church on Sunday" only may be how we practice our Christian experience, but it is not a concept that can be recognized in the Bible. Rather, the impact of a godly person during the week days on a secular job is a crucial aspect of the believer's life. The biblical believer's life is a seven day life. We all need to work, the only question is whether we should work as unto the Lord for someone else, or in our own company for ourselves.

I am aware that many Christians find it difficult to be involved in the workplace, either as an employee or as an employer. This raises a significant question and it needs to be answered. If we have a message that is practical and living and for the whole world, why would we fear walking into the territory where we have the most opportunity to be with those who also need Jesus? Is the message not real to us? If it is, we are the blessed ones to bring the heavenly overflow to thirsty souls with whom we work.

Perhaps no other human experience makes it more evident that the Christian is a child of two worlds as how he performs in the world of work.

If Christ is not real to us, perhaps this explains the fear some have of working in a place where language is bad, dispositions are crude and no one wants to hear about your Bible study. May I suggest that if we have a fear like this, the question may be more about our character than our Christianity, more about our lack of wisdom or faith than about how wrong the world is and how needy are the people in it. The cup that is full and overflowing need not be self-conscious about its refreshing effect on others. If we focus on enjoying Christ in our personal walk with the Lord, our fears will tend to melt and our conflict will turn into passion and concern for others.

Perhaps no other human experience makes it more evident that the Christian is a child of two worlds as how he performs in the world of work. Nevertheless, I think the conflict we may have about how to be in the work place is misplaced. If the apparent conflict exists because we have to choose whether to be religious or secular, that is a problem, and that would be a genuine conflict. However, that may be the wrong question and, therefore, the wrong answer.

The challenge is not religion versus secularity. The challenge, rather, is being spiritual versus being worldly. God is not about religion; He is about being alive inside a person who believes. Religion is about a set of regulations and expectations and legalistic teachings, but God is about a relationship. Knowing God this way is about enjoying His divine life while walking among our fellow man.

If we are those who walk with the Lord in a loving relationship, that is about Life, not religion. If we walk with the Lord in our daily life, in our work life, in our performance of business as a manager or self-employed person, there is no conflict. Rather, the challenge is to walk as a spiritual person in the midst of our worldly, needful duties. Take care of the life of God in you and take care of your business with those around you according to integrity and according to the laws of the land. How can there be a conflict in this?

For me, being a responsible person in the business world is not a mission to change a world under condemnation. My task is learning to live by a heavenly, divine resource, even as others around me examine my life in the midst of earthly challenges. When I am tried and found wanting, it is serious, but it is also an incentive to seek the Lord.

Ultimately, it is not I but Christ in me who is faithful and who is always ready to renew and mold my character and the decisions I make. This process is not merely a decision for one day or for one period of time. It is for my journey of life in Christ in the midst of the world as a businessman.

For many believers, the task of being in business successfully as a Christian appears daunting, if not impossible. On the contrary, my view is that there are laborato-

My task is learning to live by a heavenly, divine resource, even as others around me examine my life in the midst of earthly challenges.

ries in our daily lives in which we can practice the things of God. One of these laboratories is our work life. Other laboratories include our family life and church life, but this discussion focuses most directly on the laboratory of work. Through insurmountable challenges and failures, for me it has become a means by which God seems to find a way to make himself personal and real to me, and by extension, to my family.

So then, how can you be a "Christian boss"? The challenging question itself presumes there is an answer…yet there may not be a simple one, so I hope you will continue reading.

Part I:

You: The Person, The Worker and The Work

Out of your innermost thought and
character comes your work.
You don't just work-
what you do becomes who you are.
You don't just work-
you are the worker, and the worker in
you defines much about who you are,
how you are, and some of what you
think it means to be truly alive.

I. You: the person, the worker and the work

In each point of this discussion, it is important to start with you, the person; the person who is a Christian. Who are you? What kind of person are you? Not only do I ask what you believe, but how do you live the testimony of Christ wherever you live and work? Is it something "just in your head and heart", or has it found its way into your character, into your attitude, and into your habits and viewpoints?

Out of your identity and loving relationship with Christ come the means and motivation by which you can work and provide for your family. Some believers think that to "live by faith" is to sit around passively and wait for "God" to supply all their needs. In the Bible, that kind of "faith" is not faith. It is laziness, it is presumption and it is totally unacceptable not only to God, not only to the church, but even to the unbelieving world.

Many Christians are sincere but when they live and work it doesn't look like God lives there.

In fact, Paul speaks strongly to this point. Have you noticed this? "...if any would not work, neither should he eat!" (I Thessalonians 5:10). How about another thought on this? "But if any provide not for his own, and specially for those of his own house, *he has denied the faith and is worse than an infidel!*" (I Timothy 5:8). You can see how practical is the word of God to the believer. No work... no eat. No care for your family...you don't even deserve the fallen world!

Many Christians are sincere but when they live and work it doesn't look like God lives there. In a sense, this subject lends itself more to the practice of human living than it does to your doctrinal believing. In fact, your life at work is the public "laboratory examination" of your private "classroom beliefs". For example, there are masterful, honest, *successful unbelievers* and there are *lazy believers*; there are even sincere and hardworking bankrupt, clueless believers.

So then, to be a godly, Christian boss is not such a simple thing. It is about a believer learning to function as an adjusted, envisioned, compassionate person whose transforming motivation is God living in him. It is much more than a person with a "good character" and drive. It is someone making his own way providing for his family with a "God character" living in the midst of an unbelieving, needy, broken and crooked world.

The object of this discussion is how to provide for your family and in a godly way be successful in what you do, especially in self-employment or in management for another company. With the Lord's help, we can learn that this great challenge is a wonderful opportunity to know the Lord in our daily lives amidst the most challenging circumstances, even while providing for our families.

Who we are represents how we do things. The foregoing discussion will test "who" we are at the present time. So again I ask you, "Who are you?". Out of your innermost thought and character comes your work. You don't just work- what you do becomes who you are. You don't just work- you are the worker, and the worker in you defines much about who you are, how you are, and some of what you think it means to be truly alive.

So then, to be a godly, Christian boss is not such a simple thing. It is about a believer learning to function as an adjusted, envisioned, compassionate person whose transforming motivation is God living in him.

Part II:

Relationships

***No one actually works for himself.
Everyone answers
to someone somewhere.
Even the dictator got the breath in
his nostrils from someone else.***

II. Relationships

If you want to be self-supporting or in a position to represent and lead others, you are not among the lazy or passive. You are among those who want to *work*, want to *work hard* and want to better *learn how to work*. You are among those who want to be constituted with right thinking, diligent living and a profitable investment of your time. In the process, you want to learn how to be right with God, with your Church, with your Family, with your Work and with the World. Later in this discussion, we will add further thoughts as why I have listed these five relationships in this order.

After considering what kind of person you are, it is important to consider your relationship with each of them:

1. God

We assume here that you are a biblical Christian who really wants to walk with Jesus all day every day every place you go. If you are not such a person with such a passionate desire, may I suggest you not only underestimate God's provision for your humanity, but you deprive yourself and those around you of an uplifted life that is unattainable by anyone other than those who "know" Christ. Such a life is the result of being a "partaker of the Divine Nature" and of abiding in Christ. (II Peter 1:3-4; John 15:4-5; Romans 10:8-17).

Take care to not dissect "spiritual" from "secular" life.

If we are wrong with God, nothing we do will ever be truly right. Impressive and "good" things are done without God, but things that have both temporal and eternal value must begin and end with their source in God. Take care to not dissect "spiritual" from "secular" life. In biblical thought, there is no dissection and there is no confusing talk about "balance". For the biblical, normal believer, there is just being who you are every day in the sight of God as you walk among your fellow man. If you are "religious", you need to set aside time for your "religious life" and for your "secular life"; but, if you are a biblical believer you just "live" all day every day. (John 5:38-40).

No one is more in need of learning to live a balanced life than one who has his own business or who feels somewhat "owned" by another company. This kind of balance is a good balance. It means making time for your priorities of time alone with God, time alone with your spouse, time with your family and church people and neighbors. It means making time for your personal growth, for recreation, civic responsibilities and for other important things in daily life. It means keeping your priorities, lest the precious days of your life be given to lifeless work.

If you think you have to have a balance between your "secular" life and your "religious" life, that is a wrong kind of balance. The biblical thought is not about religion. It is not about separating your life into segments. Rather, it is about learning to walk with God as a spiritual person in the midst of all your day by day activities in the world. In all the aspects of our life, we do well to walk with God and bring the overflow of that life and that walk into all the aspects of our daily affairs.

This is about walking with God and being up-to-date with Him, all day every day whether on the job, at home, with a neighbor or in a meeting with some believers.

How can you keep priorities? How can you have a balanced life? Make time for God in the early part of your day and He will make your time well used throughout the day. (Isaiah 50:4). Even a brief time in the Bible and in prayer makes a big difference. Enjoying Christ first thing in the morning is like having a heavenly breakfast. If you eat oatmeal for breakfast, without thinking about it that little bowl of food is your strength to work hard and think about things well for hours. Likewise, feed on God and He becomes that portion of strength to meet situations throughout the hours that follow. This is not about being religious. This is about walking with God and being up-to-date with Him, all day every day whether on the job, at home, with a neighbor or in a meeting with some believers.

2. Church

A man needs a dream, but that dream needs perspective. Is loyalty to your family or to your business your first priority? While any job can be hard on a marriage and on a family, self-employment and management responsibilities inevitably bring even more challenges. Although the pressures may eventually ease, at least periodically, you must realize there will likely be more demand on your time, on your family commitments and on your finances, not less.

Let your business life be measured in the context of a committed church life and family life. This will help you keep perspective.

Let your business life be measured in the context of a committed church life and family life. This will help you keep perspective. The Lord saved you and your family for the church and for His testimony to the world, not for success in business. You can and should succeed in business, but that is not the goal of your life; it is the by-product of right living, right thinking, right commitments and of time well used.

I am thinking of a dear young couple close to our hearts that are living examples of this matter. When this young Christian man was at the university pursuing his doctorate in a most difficult field, his priorities did not change from what he had already learned. He and his wife had grown in conviction from the Lord that she should be a homemaker.

The Lord saved you and your family for the church and for His testimony to the world, not for success in business.

When they had their first child, she stopped working outside the home. Because he had learned *how* to work, he was able to get a high-paying part time job while he continued in his education full time. When he graduated from this esteemed university, his advisor wrote a letter of recommendation about him that could make a proud man blush or cry. His pickup and her car were both paid for, his many years of school were paid for, his medical bills were paid for and they had money in the bank.

Not only so, they almost never missed any meetings of the church, where they each gladly exercised responsibility to strengthen other young couples and families in the faith. She was so useful in ministries of music and he prepared and led studies in the Word of God and preached to the public. Still, it seemed they always had time to talk, to pray, to fellowship and to go out for dinner.

After only five years at a university where he is now a professor, he was asked to become the Associate Dean of the College of Arts and Sciences. He has much responsibility and many people answer to him now, but his way to handle them makes people glad to work there and know him. With such responsibility and added prestige, he and his wife continue their work as unto the Lord. She faithfully invests her days in two young children in a wonderful way, even as she expands her abilities and passion in ministries of music, publication layout and designs, discipling others, and what other things you may find in Proverbs 31.

For them, success and financial provision are the byproduct of lives set in order by the enjoyment of Christ in the faithfulness of their being-redeemed humanity.

Any of these points about this couple could be impressive in themselves, but these things could also be a distraction from things that really count in the long run. Instead, their love is for their home and their home is for the church. His studies and work fit into the context of this. Watching them live, it is quite difficult to not notice the spiritual life of Christ being displayed in their daily humanity.

While I invite you to join me and say "Wow!", I also encourage you to join me in realizing this is as "normal" as it is wonderful. They may not be "typical", but knowing Christ in such a way makes a lifestyle of work and responsibility have the perspective and impact it should have. For them, success and financial provision are the byproduct of lives set in order by the enjoyment of Christ in the faithfulness of their being-redeemed humanity. It seems the Christ they know is able to bear much responsibility and influence in a "secular" job without compromising the spiritual integrity that leads them day by day.

3. Family

I Timothy 5:8 says, "But if any provide not for his own, and specially for those of his own house, he hath denied the faith and is *worse than an infidel.*" Clearly, the spiritual life must be practical. Perhaps there is no better way for a believer to practice the faith than the way he views work and the way he works. This subject is a big one, often missed by sincere believers who are "so spiritual" they can't be bothered to work. Such a person may be somewhat deluded in thinking he is too spiritual to touch earthly things, but his family suffers because of his false spirituality. Behind such a mask may lie a misunderstanding of spirituality, fear of failure or just "plain old laziness".

Your vision of work needs to include consideration for and with your family each step of the way.

Any job well done is challenging and difficult, and that is if you work for someone else. If you decide to be your own boss or accept more responsibility where you are employed, it becomes more challenging, not less. While there are some great advantages to self-employment or promotion elsewhere, the cost of commitment, responsibility and accountability is higher.

It is important to not only provide for your family but also have your family be prepared for the challenges of your business. If possible, help them share your life in such a way they feel it is their business, too. Few people just drift into success.

Few unprepared people are able to bring their marriage and family through difficult situations without lasting damage to them.

You need a vision for your future that includes your family. You need a vision, but don't mistake wishful thinking for vision when it may instead be a romantic dream or even an escape hatch from your current employment or general situation. Your vision of work needs to include consideration for and with your family each step of the way.

4. Work

For many people today, "work" is a "four-letter word", in the sense that it is often a distasteful, negative subject. In the Bible, it was not so. One of the basic commandments given to Moses says "Six days shalt thou labor and do all thy work." In Genesis, God labored six days. Proverbs, Ecclesiastes and the Lamentations of Jeremiah are books with many thoughts about work and principles of character for daily life at work.

As a God-centered believer, the challenge is not just to work and to work hard, but to learn well how to work.

The apostle Paul wrote, "if a man will not work, neither should he eat". (II Thessalonians 3:10). Most people work, some work hard, but few ever learn *how* to work. In the same way, most boys play football, some will learn to play hard enough to be noticed, but a small number ever learn *how* to play. They are the ones who become extremely successful professionals. Some of the professionals have less talent than many who were left behind. They are the ones who didn't just sweat and work hard but they also learned *how* to get the job done.

The biblical man works, he works hard and he ought to give himself to learn *how* to work well. Self-employment and management positions often require much of the worker.

As a God-centered believer, the challenge is not just *to work and to work hard,* but to learn well *how to work.* Then comes a precaution: once you learn *how to work* you must learn *how to not be consumed by your work.* Under normal conditions, six days is a biblical model, not seven. Lazy people are content to work as little as possible.

Discipline requires diligence but wisdom and the biblical pattern also insist on limitation. Work, but pause to rest. Rest, but don't be lazy. Never is this challenge of leading a balanced life more evident than when you are responsible for everything as "the boss".

Work, but pause to rest. Rest, but don't be lazy.

5. World

It is never the right time to be mad at the world, and it is always wrong to be jealous of it or take advantage of it dishonorably. It is always the right time to be right with God and with men everywhere. If our hearts are right with God, then we have a way to walk in truth and live rightly in the world.

When Satan lives among his people, the system of the world is produced. When Christ lives among His people, the biblical church is produced. It is therefore a great challenge for a godly believer whose redeemed heart is called and designed for another kingdom to live well in this self-centered world.

Nowhere is this challenge more evident than a believer who wishes to live God's way in a business world that is bent away from God. It can be done and it should be done, but the complexity of issues seem difficult to navigate for many sincere believers. To be "in this world but not of this world" is never more difficult than for a self -employed believer or one in higher management for a company that may lack principle and integrity. Are you ready for the challenge?

It is never the right time to be mad at the world, and it is always wrong to be jealous of it or take advantage of it dishonorably. It is always the right time to be right with God and with men everywhere.

To be "in this world but not of this world" is never more difficult than for a self-employed believer or one in higher management for a company that may lack principle and integrity.

Are you ready for the challenge?

Part III:

Points of Consideration

Management should not appear threatening like a weapon. Authority should be used like an umbrella to cover those under one's care from the storm and as a platform from which to lead others in excellence by example.

III. Points of consideration

1. Identity: *who* are you, *what* kind of a person are you and *how* do you work?

We have already talked a little bit about *who* you are. Let's consider this idea a little more and add a few thoughts to it. The modern world of work is cut into specific pieces. You may have a career in hanging doors in a house but never learn to pour the foundation for it or put shingles on it. You may be a doctor and specialize in one part of the body or one disease, but never learn how to care for a frightened patient dying in the hospital.

When you decide to be a business person, there is a lot of change. It will likely include a broad spectrum of duties, not just a point of one specialty ability. Not only must you know your trade or profession well, but you must also know people, divisions of government, legal responsibilities, insurance needs, payroll or 1099 issues and a host of other matters never considered by a "9-5 employee". Suddenly, it is not just about what you can produce with your hands or your mind. It is also about what kind of person you are, what your character is like under pressure, how you deal with situations, responsibilities and public accountabilities.

You will never be able to do more or carry more responsibility than allowed by the quality and stability of your character.

The issue is now not just about what you can do or what you offer to the business community. It is very much about who you are as a person, how you think and how you work. You will never be able to do more or carry more responsibility than allowed by the quality and stability of your character.

Although there are many things to consider, the issue of *how to work* is a big point. What you learn and experience along the way in life will develop your habits and views about life in general. This general preparation will greatly affect your capabilities to perform later, specifically as a leader in business. Since I have repeatedly mentioned learning "*how* to work" as well as just "working *hard*", I would like to suggest a few principles I have learned about this and then, from my personal experience, illustrate a little more why I think this is important.

◈ **Principles of learning *how to work:***

1. *Whatever you are doing, give yourself to it wholly.*

Give it all you've got and direction will come!

If it is not worth the commitment to perfect it, it may not be worth the time to start it. A principle of life-long learning and application like this is illustrated in Ecclesiastes 9:10, "Whatsoever thy hand findeth to do, do it with thy might!" If your job is to sweep a sidewalk in bad weather, deliver a public address to a university, or read a story to your child, treat it the same.

Treat each task as though it were God's gift to you for the moment (because it is!). Out of that moment will come much more, if you are given to it. Vincent Van Gogh strengthens this thought and somewhere said, "If you master one thing and understand it well, you will also have insight and understanding of many things".

Such commitment often produces further opportunity and "leading" where to go or what to do next. The wind can never catch the sail of a ship in the harbor with its sail let down. A passive or casual commitment is like a sail at rest. Even if the wind is blowing, you will never know it or take a direction. The lazy sail will never know the trip it missed. *Give it all you've got and direction will come*! Mentors will take notice, you will be inspired and you may learn to listen to the voice of the leading Shepherd in the midst of your daily walk. (John 10:27; I Peter 5:4a).

2. *Learn to do whatever you do thoroughly; learn to multi-task broadly; and learn to focus completely on whichever task you are doing at the moment.*

This is an exercise of you being in charge of yourself instead of being whip-lashed by circumstances or new emails or telephone calls that may be important, but shouldn't distract you. What do you do if you are talking to a customer and your cell phone rings in your pocket? What if you are in the midst of responding to an email and you have a deadline to be somewhere? Can you focus? Can you make the right choice and not feel pressured or out of control?

In my earlier college years, my mind was scattered, undisciplined, and quite unable to focus. However, I had a great desire to walk with God, to learn from people and to make a difference with my life. I began to read a lot of books of many kinds and subjects. When I read a book for an hour, it was difficult to clearly recall more than one important point, so I made the decision to work on my focus and on my reading and memory capacity.

I recall choosing forty-seven books from my shelf to read. I exercised myself to read each of them for one minute so that I might have forty-seven things I could recall instead of just one at the end of about one hour. I learned to let one book's thought go and instantly focus on the next one for a page or two in the minute I had. I found that, in less than one hour, I could grasp dozens of new thoughts and ideas. This exercise greatly helped me learn to focus intensely and immediately on whatever I was reading or doing. It helped me to be occupied, but not preoccupied; active, yet focused; committed, but not in bondage; at liberty, yet not scattered.

As an extension of that practice, I learned to shift from one thing to another in my work-day with undistracted attention. This life-long exercise has been helpful. Even now as I am writing, some email notices popped up. Since I have some time-sensitive issues at hand, I intentionally glanced at the subject line of each one as it passed across the screen. There were several important ones, but none that need instantaneous response. When it is convenient, I will open them later, instead of be distracted in this section from this moment with you.

When everything seems apparently important, nothing actually is.

Why is this important? Because practical effects come out of priorities well understood. When everything seems apparently important, nothing actually is. Your life can either truly live, or you can just passively let your life happen randomly. It's up to you. The first person will help shape your company, the latter person will always work for another one.

3. ***Don't wait for someone else to teach you or help you, regarding what it is on your life's horizon.***

Seek it and pursue it when it is available from anyone anywhere, but don't wait to be spoon-fed. Take initiative. Ask the Lord to impassion you with a thirst to learn. Having no desire to read or no heart to learn in some other way is a reason, but it is not an excuse. We do well to consume the scriptures and the God of the scriptures until they consume us. There is a living fire inside the black and white words of the holy scriptures. Pray and ask the Lord to open the words until they open you. (Proverbs 2:1 -5; Jeremiah 20:9).

Don't ever say you didn't have an opportunity or take a posture where you blame others for failures, shortages or less potential in yourself or your situation. Galileo Galilei somewhere said "You cannot teach a man anything. You can only help him discover it for himself". If you have a heart to learn, there will be no lack of available assistance or encouragement by others who wish to impart their hearts into someone who in himself is passionate and forward looking. Bottom line: it is your life: you choose, you act, you make it happen, you be the one seeking to discover instead of being the one to passively let "luck" come to you.

Bottom line: it is your life: you choose, you act, you make it happen, you be the one seeking to discover instead of being the one to passively let "luck" come to you.

The Bible begins by saying "In the beginning, God created...". Instead of that beautiful, inspiring beginning, what if it said, "In the beginning, God just sat around to see what might happen someday..."? It is unthinkable for Him, and it ought to be unthinkable for us. To know God is to really live! To be passive in our lazy self is to waste the only thing we truly have: His purpose and our time.

4. ***Look beyond the task at hand.***

Learning is not just about gathering information. Learning is about grasping ideas, principles, new and large thoughts. If you see a certain task as unnecessary, unrelated or a waste of time, you have gotten out of God and into knowledge for as long as you are there. When you touch God, experience grows. When you touch knowledge as dead information, it is like a storm without a rainbow or a body without a breath. If a task is just a task, its importance is lost. If you see it as a part of the whole realm of life and learning and purpose and hope, the smallest thing can become like a crucial, small piece of a large puzzle that would be incomplete without it. Look at the whole, not the part. Enjoy the parts and grasp the whole until that is who you are.

5. *Refuse to let ordinary things make your life ordinary.*

Let the necessities of each day be always new and meaningful and purposeful. For example, sometimes when I look in the mirror while I shave, I have the inner thought that there is much in me that needs trimming and cut off. If I take out the trash, sometimes I may be impressed to open to the Lord and ask him to empty me, unload me of all the things in my life that are just rubbish.

If I look in the refrigerator to see what Christine may have bought for us, when I see the peaches and the blueberries, it may inspire me to turn my heart to the Lord and ask Him to make me fruitful in my life, in my home, in my business and in the church.

If we lose such freshness, we may "die" many years before we retire or stop breathing altogether. Abraham Lincoln is said to have remarked that what will really matter, in the end, is not how many were the years of your life, but of how much life was in your years.

Abraham Lincoln is said to have remarked that what will really matter, in the end, is not how many were the years of your life, but of how much life was in your years.

6. *Ask the Lord for a diligence in your spirit, in your soul and in your body.*

Don't just work at it and don't just become a hard worker. While you are pursuing, ask the Lord to show you *how to learn from each situation and make that the new, up-to-date "you"*. Let each situation be seen firstly as an opportunity before you embrace it as a responsibility. Never consider yourself as being in a box (unless you are, in which case you need to deal with it), and never let others put you in one. Sometimes I hear a challenge from someone "to think outside the box". My only question is, "Where did the box come from?".

Let each situation be seen firstly as an opportunity before you embrace it as a responsibility.

Yes, in a sense, we always are measured by and against others. That's how the Olympian will know he broke a world record, because he won the race against others. However, as part of his training, he learned that his greatest competitor is himself. If he measures himself against himself, winning the race against others will largely take care of itself. Medal or no medal in daily life, public honor or no honor, contract or no contract, if you live and do all things heartily "as unto the Lord", the reward lies in itself and in God, not in the words of others. (Colossians 3:23). This is a hard lesson to learn and to keep learning, but ultimately, that is really what matters.

7. ***Learn to use your time well.***

Work intentionally and rest intentionally. Enjoy momentum, but know when to stop. If your day is well used, let the pressures of the day end before the day ends.

Let me ask you some related things: If your time is focused, what do you do if you have five minutes or three or twelve minutes before you need to do something else? Can you spend a focused minute or two or six with your wife, a worker or a reading project? Can you write an email in a minute or five instead of wasting that time? If you can, then can you disengage from that task instantly and move on, undistracted, to the next thing?

The only thing you actually own is your time. Do you own it, or does it own you?

Can you come home in a way your family will be glad you did? Or, do you come home preoccupied, brow wrinkled and oblivious to the one(s) who love you and pray for you throughout the day? As an extension of this, if you have a day or a vacation period away from your work, can you leave everything at home or at the office so you are freed in mind and heart, and not just drag it with you to a different place?

The only thing you actually own is your time. Do you own it, or does it own you? Virtually no matter what else fails or causes bankruptcy or is broken or hurt, it can be possibly replaced or recovered eventually. Not so with your time. A minute lost is a wasted investment in a gray hair that can never be earned, explained or compensated. Walk with God in a way that He becomes the active figure in your life. Then you can spend your day acting instead of reacting.

My endeavor to learn these principles of *how to work*

Preparation in my own work experience may be a small example of the guidelines I have just proposed. Although my exposure in self-employment began at age eight, mowing a lawn across the street for Mrs. Graham, I will fast-forward to the days when I left home north of Denver for a small school in Chicago.

I had not done very well in high school and I also had no idea how to make a friend or be a friend. When I left for school, I desired a great change. In my first semester of college, I took a full load of 16 units. I devoted myself to school, and nothing but school. I studied, and I studied hard. I still have my calendar where I recorded the number of hours I spent studying each subject day by day. In my first semester of Greek, I studied as many as thirty hours a week in that class alone. My final grade was a "C", just average.

I was learning to study and to study hard, but I didn't know *how* to study well. By the end of my first semester, my life savings was gone, so I worked as a dish washer in the school cafeteria. I had to work more each semester to avoid debt and pay my way as I went. By the second year, I was a cook in the cafeteria and also traveled to Lutheran Hospital in downtown Chicago to mop floors several nights a week and on holidays.

I was learning to study and to study hard, but I didn't know how to study well.

As an added factor, I had begun learning to enjoy my classmates and was much involved with class offices and many activities at school. Because I worked a lot and was involved in some twenty-two extra-curricular activities my second year, I had time to study considerably less, but still got an "A" in Greek. I had learned much about *how* to study, a step quite improved from just studying *hard*. Smarter? I think not, only more diligent and focused in how my time was used.

After two years at Trinity College in Chicago, I transferred to CSC for four years (University of California at Chico). During my first semester of graduate work, I gained approval to take nine classes, totaling 25 units, nearly a full years worth of work. In addition to the school studies, there were other things on my schedule. I was also a student assistant in Psychology for Dr. Hugh M. Bell, the delightful and world famous psychologist. He asked me to work with him and that took a lot of time making up exams for my classmates, (they never knew), and grading them for him. I spent about twenty hours a week on campus sharing the gospel with my fellow students in Bible studies, working with the Navigators, Inter-Varsity and Campus Crusade. I was also a "dorm dad", which was a great opportunity to care for both the school's concerns and my classmates' needs.

Still, I got adequate sleep and had ample time to go hunting for pheasants and ducks with Billy, my friend who lived on a rice farm south of town. During that particular semester, I kept account of my study time and discovered I could only allow for as little as five hours a week on my studies, ordinarily what would be expected from one class; and I had nine classes. Not because I was suddenly "bright", but because I was learning *how* to study and use my time well, I went into the finals with an "A" average. I graduated with honors, having a major in Psychology; and two teaching minors- in Speech and Drama; and the Industrial Arts, specializing in Electricity / Electronics, Auto shop and Wood shop.

If we learn how to "dig in deeply into the moment", we learn general knowledge and experience that prepare us for specific things to come later.

We are all different in many ways, but we are probably all the same in one way. We all have some kind of situation year after year that is bigger than we are. At times, it seemed I had every reason to give up and never try to use my life well, except I knew God had touched me deeply in junior high school and that love affair with Him became my prime motivation.

Especially before going away to college, my character was full of holes. At times, it seemed I did not know how to be with people nor did I have capacity to care too much what happened to them. My high school principal belittled me publicly and told me plainly I would never amount to anything. I passed Geometry with a D- in his class, only out of his respect for my mother, who was a great grade school teacher in the school system. He was probably right about me at the time. I did not study very much at all, I did not know how to study and I didn't think about asking anybody to help me. I was lonely, empty and childish to the day I left for college.

This difficulty of *knowing how to be alive* seemed to swallow my whole life at the time. Eventually, it helped me to learn something. You may have a similar experience of learning from a hard time. If we learn how to "dig deeply into the moment", we will learn general knowledge and experience that prepares us for specific things to come later. As to our topic here, if you wish to own a company or lead in management, what you have been willing to learn along the way is preparing you as a whole person to be committed to your big task in the business world.

So, you want to be

A Christian boss...

Why?

2. Motive for making a change

So you want to be your own boss now, and/or perhaps the boss of others as well? The first question I want to ask you is "Why?". If you are not clear on this point you will waste a lot of time and perhaps get seriously sidetracked in your life's direction. I have seen and heard several interesting things that are "reasons" for being self-employed, or accepting more managerial responsibility than one might be prepared for. Sincere and genuine Christian believers seem to be vulnerable to the most severe mistakes.

Let me list a few reasons I have heard for going into business and see if any of them might be true of you. In my view, only one of them is reasonable, practical and makes sense in our world today as believers. What is your view?

1. *You could control your own schedule and have a lot of free time for your family.*
2. *You could make a lot of money for God and support missionaries all over the world.*
3. *You could hire other believers and help them with their financial troubles.*
4. *You could partner with another(s) brother in the Lord and have a lot of time on the job to pray together and win your customers and employees to Christ.*
5. *You could be a testimony to the dark business world that Jesus has made you "different".*
6. *You could escape all the hassle of working for "ungodly bosses" and for "companies that are unrighteous".*
7. *You could get rich, retire early and have the rest of your life "free for God".*
8. *You could hire people that no one else understands. This would be a witness of God's love for them, "so they might get saved because of your kindness".*
9. *You could give discounts to Christians who would be your clients. This would be a spiritual blessing to them and help them in their financial sufferings. They might tell other people about your company and bring more business to you. Since you have such a pure motive, even if you lost money God would understand and take care of you somehow.*
10. *You are skilled and prepared in a trade or profession and have good business sense. Your family is supportive and understands the risks and is committed with you to face at least two years of extreme challenges to time and finances. You have peace with God and it seems good to those who know you best, especially spiritual brothers with practical sense. There is every reason to conclude this is the Lord's leading for you as the best way to provide for your family and for your long term goals in life.*
11. *What are your expectations?*

3. Why accept a promotion or start your own business?

The previous section on motive is about your intention, about why you are considering having your own company. *Purpose* is about your goal in starting the company or receiving management responsibility where you now work. If you proceed, what do you want to see happen? What are your financial goals? What are your minimum expectations and your long term plans? What benefits do you plan for in terms of time invested, flexibility of schedule, minimum income and profit potentials? If you do poorly, will that affect what is in your heart for your family, for your time availability with them and for the church and for other ministry? If things go badly, are you prepared to blame yourself instead of God or someone else?

Matthew 6:33 says "Seek ye first the Kingdom of God and all these things shall be added unto you." What does this verse mean to you in regard to your purpose as a person on the front line of the business world? Can you seek "Jesus only" while you are involved in your work so intensely? Is your spirit free to pray and seek God while your mind and body are attentive to your responsibilities and goals in your business?

Is your spirit free to pray and seek God while your mind and body are attentive to your responsibilities and goals in your business?

I was once in business with two other Christian brothers as a corporation. We were awarded huge construction contracts right after I was first licensed as a general contractor. We hired many "brothers" as carpenters. One of them was a fellow elder in the church. His view of being an employee and my view of having one were very different. He thought the job was a place for him to express his spirituality by preaching to others, not doing the job for which he was hired. He repeatedly would be screaming "spiritual things" at the top of his lungs for all the unbelieving workers to hear all over the large construction site. He caused a great distraction and his work was not particularly good. He was so busy being "spiritual" that it was costing my company a lot of money to put up with his low production and distraction to others. I finally instructed one of my partners to tell him to be quiet and get to work or he would be fired!

There were a number of other "brothers" working for me during that same period of time. They had read in Acts 2:44-45 that "the believers had all things in common". They liked that verse. They felt that the proceeds of the contracts should be evenly divided with them. I quickly learned how strange their concept was if it was imposed on business matters.

In addition to working on the job all day, I was the one who had had been qualified to obtain a General Contractors License, had endless responsibilities and liabilities, paper work for the government, invoices to pay; and it was my company. These issues took much extra time. Additionally, I borrowed money to buy all the equipment for the projects and serviced the equipment and the debts. When an expensive saw was stolen or other things cost a lot of money and took extra time, I had to pay, but the workers wanted the financial benefit of the work if we made money, because they were "Christian brothers".

God's governing principle is about Christ and the Church. The world is about a controlling principle based on currency. No work, no pay. Little work, little pay. Much work, much pay.

From such experiences as these, I quickly realized there are two economies. God's economy is about the life and experience of Christ that God invests in His believers and works on them for an eternal building. Christ is the life, Christ is the goal, Christ is the currency and Christ is the Way to become part of God's divine corporation for eternity.

The other economy is that of the world economy, and it is based on material currency. While a believer should realize he has a redeemed and uplifted humanity, he should never use it to take advantage of the world in the process. God's governing principle is about Christ and the Church. The world is about a controlling principle based on currency. No work, no pay. Little work, little pay. Much work, much pay.

I quickly learned the difference between the governing principle of Christ and the governing principle of material currency. As a result, I made a decision to never hire a person "just because he is a brother" in the Lord. My guiding principle quickly became, "I don't hire brothers, I hire carpenters". If I have a choice, I always would choose a brother, but that choice is based on his skill, not on his religious views or affiliation.

Is this thought troublesome to you? If so, let me ask you a question. If you were going to have a major surgery facing a life or death matter, which surgeon would you choose? If you had only two choices, would you choose a medical student with no experience but who is a Christian? Or, would you choose an atheistic, anti-government surgeon who is a dependable human being with a great track record for decades as a world-class professional surgeon?

Another example. Suppose you own an airplane but you are not a pilot. Would you hire a pilot for your trip because he is "a Christian brother" who just got his license last week? Or, would you hire an unbeliever who is a seasoned, skilled pilot, who has survived many harrowing experiences because of his skill, his track record and his calmness in troubling situations?

In the business world, I am subject to the rules of that system. If I impose some "religious" evaluations on it, things invariably become impractical, clouded and confused.

In these examples, I have a hard time thinking any logical person would choose spiritual standing over practical, tested skills. In the same principle, I learned to hire skill and disposition, not an unlearned man just because he is "in the faith". For me, there is no conflict in this. Rather, it would be foolish to try providing for my family in such a compromising fashion. In the business world, I am subject to the rules of that system. If I impose some "religious" evaluations on it, things invariably become impractical, clouded and confused.

Keep it simple. In God's economy, build up the saints in the church. In the world's economy as a business man, build up the business using the virtues, attributes and skills you have learned along the way. If it is a matter of fellowship, open your Bible. If it is a matter of business, open your check book. In either situation, always open your heart.

Jesus spoke to this issue clearly, saying "And the lord commended the unjust steward because he had done wisely: for the children of this world are in their generation wiser than the children of light. And I say unto you, Make to yourselves friends of the mammon of unrighteousness..."; and again, Solomon (not Warren Buffet or Bill Gates) said "...but money answers all things". (Luke 16:8-9; Ecclesiastes 10:19).

So then, what is your purpose in the business world? Your view will determine everything. Someone may go to the top of the mountain where they can see unparalleled beauty and clear air for perhaps a hundred miles. Someone else may do the same thing and think only about how cold it is without a coat and he can't wait to leave.

Circumstances do not change you. Your reaction to them is what shapes you, changes you and determines the result.

Actions are needed, but reactions announce what you really think and see. Your view determines the course you set and the direction you will take. You can never produce well what you have not seen and you will never see fully what you have not been willing to do practically.

4. Integrity in your character and in your work

Victory is not about what happens when there is no temptation. Victory is about what happens when temptations are there and you rise above them and walk on top of them.

Victory is not about what happens when there is no temptation. Victory is about what happens when temptations are there and you rise above them and walk on top of them. No matter how strong you are morally, no matter how committed you are ethically, no matter how well you were trained as a child or as a believer in the church, the business world inevitably brings a major assault against everything in your transformed constitution. If you don't understand this, if you don't learn how to walk with God in the midst of challenging situations, your integrity and your character will likely be dented and dismantled little by little, if not all at once. The larger your public exposure in business, the larger the situations that will need your proper attention.

It would seem that truthfulness, honesty and a fair viewpoint are all that are needed to walk righteously, whether at home, in the church life or in the business world. However, experience has taught me there is more involved, and various places in the scriptures indicate that things are not always so "black and white". I sometimes make a little joke that for many years I was so "straight, legalistic and rigid" that I had hinges installed on my knees so I could bend over to lay a ceramic tile floor, or even to pray. I imagined a little world where all is simple and clear. Little did I know what was waiting for me when I needed to engage in many new things to provide for my family in my business. The following verses and some fellowship with other experienced believers along the way has helped me much, so far. For example:

1. Ecclessiastes 7:16, "Be not righteous overmuch". What does this mean? We should not be unrighteous, but we should not be self-righteous on any level. In practical living, it is difficult to make decisions sometimes about what to do. Being legalistic may become a substitute for knowledge and wisdom. If you don't understand this, you will be so extreme in your view of integrity you will not be able to do business wisely or profitably. This is not to say integrity is sacrificed to gain profit. It is the Bible's enlightenment that helps us understand the difference between righteous and too-righteous, or self-righteous.

Being legalistic may become a substitute for knowledge and wisdom.

By the way, this principle is helpful in other ways, too. Before I was married, an older brother who had young children told me something I have never forgotten. He said, "Richard, as a parent it is my responsibility to hold my children accountable *for everything I see* them do that is wrong. But Richard, *I found out I don't have to 'see' everything*!" As a result, he was free from legalism and from governing his home coldly. He could train his children with love according to the measure of training for which they were ready. Decades later, his children and grandchildren are living testimonies of his wisdom in the Lord.

As a young man, I had a great dream and passion to serve the Lord full time with a wonderful organization of Christians. I had passed through many tests in circumstances with them for several years and had been increasingly useful to them. I had matured much in my spiritual passions, had earned their trust in practical matters and was given increasing measures of responsibility among them in ministry. After graduating from college, I was asked to spend a full year at their headquarters, a large step to full time work among them. During that summer I was the leading kitchen chef with a dream assignment, sent to a marvelous place to work with youth.

In the process of receiving those who registered for one of the weeks, I discovered a sign posted that indicated the maximum number of campers that were allowed to be in that location. I learned that a few extra campers were registered to come and I felt devastated by what appeared to me to be a break with integrity on the part of "this Christian organization". At that stage of my life, I didn't understand it was a theoretical problem, not a real one. That number was not unimportant but it was no doubt somewhat arbitrary. The leadership there had learned by experience that there were usually cancellations that kept them from over-booking, not unlike airlines do today.

Because of that very small theoretical matter I severed my commitment to them and gave up everything I thought the Lord had wanted me to do up to that point. The consequences were both deep and wide. Because of that decision, which I now consider to be absolutely ridiculous and absurd, my life was forever changed, for better or for worse I don't know. My ultra-legalistic, self-imposed standard cost both them and me much.

Over-zealous youthfulness had told me the issue was about a legalistic, presumptuous integrity; older wisdom taught me it was about learning how to live God's way, and that way will never sacrifice genuine integrity.

When I made that decision, the brother who had been an immense help to me didn't try to change my mind. With pain in his eyes, he just said, "Rich, it's going to take you a long time". And it did. When I went into business for myself years later, I learned quickly what he meant and that lesson eventually became greatly helpful to me and to others. Over-zealous youthfulness had told me the issue was about a legalistic, presumptuous integrity; older wisdom taught me it was about learning how to live God's way, and that way will never sacrifice genuine integrity.

Can you identify with this experience which I had? How have you handled such situations in the past and how will you handle them in the future? If it were you "in my shoes", how would you have handled the conflict which I felt about the question of integrity? It may seem like a small circumstance with a big question, but for me it was a "fork in the road".

What made it particularly difficult for me was that I later realized I had been utterly wrong, yet the road I had taken could not be reversed. Yes, I believe in the sovereignty of God, do you? But, in the struggle I discussed here, did I "force God to be sovereign" in a way that He might have preferred otherwise, had I been in wisdom and not in judgmental legalism?

After forty-six years, although my relationship continues warmly with this organization and with my Christian brothers who were part of that situation, my life was changed forever in ways that I will never know. Their lives, too, have been a little different because I was not directly part of them. I am forgiven by them and by the Lord, but something was lost forever because of my youthful misunderstanding. Not only so, perhaps something was gained forever, because the sovereign Christ we know is full of mercy and kindness and forever making a new way to have a fresh walk with Him. If so, it may be more about the journey than the destination. In ten or fifty years, what will your story be?

In self-employment or management there will be more than a few such decisions to make. That brings us to the next verses...

2. Romans 14:22-23, "Hast thou faith? Have it to thyself before God. Happy is he that condemneth not himself in that thing which he alloweth. And he that doubted is damned if he eat, because he eateth not in faith; for whatsoever is not of faith is sin."

Contrary to the religious mind and contrary to many assumptions in actual life, not everything is "black or white".

Contrary to the religious mind and contrary to many assumptions in actual life, not everything is "black or white". Many very important things are in the world of gray. The religious mind screams "this is compromise!". Wisdom and experience have learned otherwise. The first gathers information, the second has learned how to live a pure life in a defiled world.

This verse helps us realize that every person is different and has different convictions. If something is a matter of the law, we need to pay attention to it; but, if it is a matter of personal opinion that may be another matter.

This is not an excuse to sin or to do something illegal. This is the wisdom of God in the scriptures to help us live according to Christ, according to permissible flexibilities and according to the wisdom of God "in the midst of a crooked and perverse generation".

This kind of situation is sometimes not so simple. For example, I knew a sister in the Lord, decades ago, who was speeding on the highway, when she was stopped by the police. While being firm with her, the officer was very kind to her. He said he would not give her a ticket but warned her about improving her driving habits.

We should not be dishonest or evasive, but can we be too-righteous?

Instead of expressing gratitude for his merciful appraisal and receiving his exhortation, she did something else. She informed him that "according to the Bible", he was an officer of the law and was appointed to his position in the civic law by God. She told him he was supposed to keep the law and had failed to do so. She demanded that he immediately write a speeding ticket for her.

What do you think about this situation? Which was right? Was he? Was she? Neither? Both? Black and white area, or gray? Can you think of other situations in business where a good intention might be too conscientious? We should not be dishonest or evasive, but can we be too-righteous? (Ecclesiastes 7:16-17).

What if you have a responsibility to a Building Codes inspector who trusts you and gives you permission to move into your house, even though a handrail didn't pass Codes' inspection when he came? What if he is personally sympathetic with you and signs the legal document that says the house is approved so you can move in? After all, you convinced him you would have the handrail adjusted to meet the City's standards immediately, if he would just trust you. He had heard your plea for his leniency because your loan application and interest rate that you could afford would expire the next day. What is your stance then? He said he trusted you to make the repair and that you did not need to call him back to inspect it. Will you keep your word and confirm his trust in you? Was he wrong in his leniency as a member of the citizens' government, or did he represent the government well in building confidence and friendliness with its business community?

You need not live long, and you won't be in business for yourself very long before such issues come your way frequently. If the examples are not from your business world, be assured they still matter. They are personal decisions and you bring who you are as a person to the business world. Your circumstances and your decisions will only reflect who you really are on the inside of yourself. What will you do?

Your circumstances and your decisions will only reflect who you really are on the inside of yourself. What will you do?

3. I John 3:20-21, "For if our heart condemn us, God is greater than our heart, and knoweth all things. Beloved, if our heart condemn us not, then have we confidence toward God."

These verses are similar in thought to those in the preceding point. Although they apply to every part of a believer's God-seeking, pure life, they certainly are useful when in the business world. Sometimes decisions need to be made but it is just not clear what to do.

Whether due to being insensitive to the leading of the Spirit (Romans 8:14; Galatians 5:16, 24-25; Romans 8:5-6), or some other reason, there seem to be times when being at peace with the Lord and just not feeling condemned in my conscience is what I need to know. As long as I am not breaking the law or doing something contrary to Scripture, and I also have an inward peace, that is adequate for my guidance.

According to these verses, why is this? Because God knows all and He is not condemning the consideration or decision in my conscience. It seems right, it feels right and it seems like a reasonable decision, so it is apparently "ok". Isn't the Word of God wonderful?!

Sometimes decisions need to be made but it is just not clear what to do.

5. Priorities in life, of which your business is only a part

When the order of our priorities is God, Church, Family and Work, we have opportunity to have a holistic lifestyle that is in harmony with all things human and divine.

What is the most important thing in the world to a biblical Christian? Without doubt, it is Christ and the Church (Ephesians 3:8-11; 5:21-33). Whoaaaaa! You may say this is a strange thought and leaves out the family. You may have always heard the priorities in order are: Family, God, Work and Church. That is an American culture effort at life, but it is not the biblical approach. Since this discussion is not a Bible study, per se, I will keep this brief, but I think it is important.

The book of Ephesians is particularly broad and all encompassing in touching human life and relationships of the believer to God. This book in the Bible does touch the "big four", family, God, work and church. However, the book clearly portrays the broad stroke of God's design as Christ and the church, summarized particularly in Ephesians 5:33. In the same context it is beautifully illustrated how marriage and the family is part of the church life, as well as what one does.

By my own experience with my wife and family, we have wonderfully experienced how making Christ (our personal and practical relationships with Him) and the Church (the context and purpose and value in our daily living) the basis of our lives. When this is clearly understood, we can realize how to take care of our family and our work. The church is for our family and our family is for the church. Likewise, my work is in the context of being a value to my family and to the church.

My work is for something, especially my family and is a blessing financially to the Church. The Church gives meaning to life, especially to my family and my business life. When the order of our priorities is God, Church, Family and Work, we have opportunity to have a holistic lifestyle that is in harmony with all things human and divine. None are neglected, all is in perspective and peace reigns in our home life and business life. By this way we can be faithful in meetings of the church, enriched in our home life and have perspective in our business life. This is not a doctrinal statement so much as a testimony of the faithfulness of God to me and my family through the years.

Again, this lifestyle includes a picture of family life and business life in the context of the church life. If we will learn what this means from a biblical perspective it will be a great help. All of our lives as believers should be lived in this context. Christ is our life and the Church is our living. If we understand this, we will know how to take care of our spouse and children in the best way. Similarly, if we understand this, we will know how to order and commit our time for business affairs. If natural and earthly demands of family and finances consume us, we will lose focus, mix priorities and lose our direction.

Furthermore, the very thing we wish to accomplish may lose value and hurt our family. If we bring Christ and the Church to our family and our business arrangements, everything will have a healthy perspective and be taken care of the safest and most blessed way. I can't think of any way I have not been tested in these points, especially during business affairs, and I must confess that the biblical perspective of the four priorities wins: Christ, Church, Family, Business.

Of course, our situations are all different, our circumstances change and stages of our readiness and growth are fluid. Our priorities are our standard and aim, not our legalistic and destructive masters. As we walk with the Lord, as we are in fellowship with our spouse and family and as we are in fellowship with believers in the church whom we trust and who have our best interests at heart, we will learn how to live, how to be and how to become. In this healthy domain, self-employment can grow in the most fertile soil.

My work is for something, especially my family, and is a blessing financially to the Church.

---

6. Goals in business

So, you want to provide for your family by self-employment? Or, perhaps you work elsewhere and have opportunity for more responsibility and promotions in the company? Although you may dream that this venture will take less time and give more flexibility, it is usually quite the opposite, at least for a long time.

When I was a little guy about eight years old, I remember sitting on a stool at the counter beside my self-employed dad at Cottonwood Inn, a little hole-in-the-wall eating place beside Highway 85 in the little country town where we lived, half way between Cheyenne and Denver.

For some reason, I can still visualize one of those little signs on the wall on the wide mirror behind the counter. The sign read, "If you work hard eight hours a day, don't worry. By-and-by you will be the boss, work fourteen hours a day and have all the worries". To a child, that seemed like a cute thought. As an adult with over thirty years in business it was perhaps clever, but not cute; for me it became a stark reality where countless fourteen-hour days were short days.

There is no indicator in the Bible that money is implicitly evil in itself, although when you touch it you tend to be steered away from God, unless your heart is really free of its tentacles.

Let me suggest a few points for you to consider:

1. *Your basic responsibility is to provide for your family.* To not do so is to "deny the faith" and be "worse than an infidel". (I Timothy 5:8).

2. *What is in your heart is severely tested by dreams of financial gain.* There is no indicator in the Bible that money is implicitly evil in itself, although when you touch it you tend to be steered away from God, unless your heart is really free of its tentacles. Listen to the Word of God on this matter, "For the *love* of money is the root of all evil, which while some coveted after, they have (wandered away) from the faith and pierced themselves through with many sorrows". (I Timothy 6:10).

3. *To be in business involves not only working directly for people and working with people, but having people work for you.* Even if you intend to hire no one but do all the work for yourself, there are many things that will require the service of others. How you treat people not only reveals what kind of person you are, but it will directly affect your success as a businessman or manager.

How you treat people not only reveals what kind of person you are, but it will directly affect your success as a businessman or manager.

James 4:1-4 is a scathing exposure of how "the rich" typically misuse both money and their workers. I have hired hundreds of people over a span of more than thirty years in construction, development and real estate sales. It has ever been a challenge to me to pay people fairly, so at the end of every pay period and project my helpers are content.

That doesn't mean I'm soft, it means I have asked the Lord to make me a man who is fair. For example, I have "fired" some workers, but not too many. One time in 1982, I hired a carpenter who brought much turmoil to relationships on the job. When he had asked me for a job I told him what the wage would be. He got very angry and said "When I work for the union I make over $20 and hour and you will pay me $11?!

I asked him a question or two and he sheepishly replied that the union only kept him busy about three months a year. I said, "My helpers have work all year long. If your union is so wonderful, why are you knocking on my door?" He took the job, but from the beginning he was a belligerent and troublesome worker. I spoke to him about his attitude and inappropriate words more than once.

One day, I knew he could no longer be tolerated in my wealthy customer's home, behaving like he did. When I spoke with him and handed him his check, he thanked me for the opportunity to work for me. He said I had treated him so fairly and he deserved to be fired. That kind of response under the circumstances was an encouragement to me. It confirmed to me what I always tried to do while I was trying to earn a good living to provide for my family. Sometimes I had to make very difficult decisions about costs and wages and subcontractor prices, but I was in business, and that is part of it. In the midst of the heat of things, I learned I could always be fair. I was not taking advantage of my workers' skills and time.

4. *What other goals do you have? Be realistic and take a step at a time.* Proceed slowly in growing your business. Depending on what kind of business you intend to have will govern many decisions you need to make up front. Do not passively assume "everything will work out". Rather, assume nothing will work out and then plan for the worst results. If you learn to plan for the low time, the regular and high times will take care of themselves. You may say this is pessimistic, but I would contend with you that it is otherwise.

Having been "in the midst of the fire" for so long, I am not concerned whether it is pessimistic or optimistic. It is important to be realistic, and this viewpoint is exactly that. Whether in the stock market, ministry, married life or here in business commitments, there may be some high points, but there will always be low points. Plan for minimal survival in the low points and enjoy the high ones as a bonus of good planning and fortunate timing. As a believer, it is a great incentive to stay attached more to the reality of Christ in you than the material stuff around you. When things get tough, which one will you prefer? Which one will guide your decisions? Your Lord, or your stuff? Spiritual liberty or material weight?

Seek the Lord's leading and pray as though it all depends on Him; and work wisely, hard and faithfully as though it all depends on you.

It is important to give your decision(s) "all you've got". At the same time, what is your Plan B in case things just do not work well for you in your business venture or promotion? Do not confuse faith with vain hope. Seek the Lord's leading and pray as though it all depends on Him; and work wisely, hard and faithfully as though it all depends on you. In the end, you may discover both aspects are parts of the same thing.

Take care to not just "stumble" into self-employment or higher management. Consider the process as carefully and seriously as you did when courting your wife or husband. It is important, it is serious and the cost must be counted beforehand to minimize the risk of a failure. Pray much, seek the wisdom of God in the scriptures, and fellowship with older and wiser believers who have passed through your proposed experience already. Be open to the Lord and to others, especially your spouse and family, but in the end know it is a hard decision for which you are ultimately responsible.

7. Money: the greatest test of how you think and live

Business. Money. Two inseparable things. Here we go again. Is money evil? Is it wrong to make a lot of money? Should a believer give away everything he makes except what he and his family need to survive? Will money make you worldly? Will money lead you astray? Do you have to be poor to be spiritual? If you are *not* poor, are you worldly? If you are poor, are you spiritual? If your tires are not bald and your house doesn't need paint, aren't you just another greedy man of the world?

Money can't make you do anything. Money is not the problem, money is the test.

Actually, money and nice things are not the problem. Money can't make you do anything. Money is not the problem, money is the test. When money comes it causes a reaction in us. What we do with it only reveals what was living in our heart before it had a reason and the power through money to do something about it. Money doesn't make you greedy, but it may expose the greed that was already there.

These are good questions, but perhaps not the right ones. I have seen both poor and wealthy men with tender hearts, faithful service, successful companies and Christ-centered living. I have seen both poor and wealthy people who are distracted by money and unable to release themselves to thankfully accept their circumstances and trust Christ to be the center of their living and provision.

Your situation may be beyond your control. Your reaction to it is not.

You may be either poor or rich and live in fear. You may be either poor or rich and live in peace. *Your situation may be beyond your control. Your reaction to it is not.* You can choose. Angry or thankful? Fearful or peaceful? That part depends on you. It depends on how you deal with our heart and with the Lord. Are you at peace today? Are you making decisions, with the Lord's leading, that will help you continue walking in peace in twenty years?

It seems our view of money is about our heart. I think it is our reaction to circumstances on the outside of us which reveals who we are on the inside. Money is not the problem itself, money is the test of our secret desires. If you have a 9-5 simple job, you may worry constantly about money but be limited in your distractions because you are limited in your ability to have more money. Thoughts creep in. You may begin to think that if you work for yourself, dreams of success will be fulfilled. You may imagine that no amount of work or time invested will be too much, if only you can accomplish your dream of being financially successful. After all, couldn't you "live for God" better if you had a lot of free time and didn't have to worry so much about the rent this month?

If you take care of Christ first, perspective and understanding of money will begin to develop in your thinking.

Such thoughts must be reckoned with and distraction from the Lord is always a present danger. Even with the best intentions, if you are the boss or have a lot of responsibility, it seems you just cannot avoid spending far more time and energy than you ever imagined. Your actions and your intentions seem to be clear, but your reactions to opportunity will determine everything. If you can learn to know the Lord's leading as the Spirit of Christ within you, you will live in peace. Follow Him, and He will take care of your needs. If you take care of Him first, perspective and understanding of money will begin to develop in your thinking. (Romans 8:14; Matthew 6:33).

8. Disposition: What are you like?

What kind of person are you? Apart from divine lessons in your experience as a believer, your disposition will rule you. Unless you learn to be led by the Word of God and the Spirit of God, you will be, at least to a large degree, a captive of your own natural "wiring".

You may have great skills with your hands or mind, but perhaps not know how to talk with people. You may be great with people but have no business sense whatsoever. You may have great skills, great business sense and a clear direction in life and want to start your own company or become the school superintendent or CEO where you are. You have the perfect disposition, the right education and financial backing.

But, what if you ask the Lord what is His leading for you in your business considerations and He says "No" to what you hope to do? You have passion, but no peace. Who will win? Can you trust God's economy of divine life and peace within you as to how you will spend your life in the world's material economy?

In a word, I want to suggest that some people are just not "wired" to work for themselves as the boss.

On the other hand, what if you would like to be self-employed or have more responsibility in management elsewhere, but you are not good at it? You have peace to pursue it, but the result is stress, financial failure, time badly used, etc. Now what? In a word, I want to suggest that some people are just not "wired" to work for themselves as the boss. Many people, do much better working for another company, where their skills are better rewarded, their time invested doesn't get out of control and they have some financial limitations, provisions and legitimate expectations.

Most people need more than natural desire or spiritual inspiration to step into the business world. While these aspects are important, you need to consider, realistically, what your experience, skills and passions are. As I've asked before, who are you? What are your abilities? What are you doing to perfect your skills with both your job technicalities and with people? Do not just dream about drifting out of nothing into something wonderful. Be active, but not unrealistic. Be courageous, but not foolish. Proclaim vision, but only if you actually have one.

Be active, but not unrealistic. Be courageous, but not foolish. Proclaim vision, but only if you actually have one.

If you start your own business or gain higher opportunity in management elsewhere, do not be proud. If you choose to remain less distracted in your job arrangement "just as an employee", do not be ashamed. As believers, we do well to not think of success in a worldly way. For us, success is being among the rare people who actually have inward peace and live a life of peace with our family, with others and provide faithfully for our family wherever we are.

9. Professional atmosphere in your business relationships

As clean air provides an atmosphere where people can live and work in optimum health, so does "atmosphere" in a work place. You are the boss. Whether you are the entire company and work directly for customers and hire no one, or you have many employees or people under your management, it is up to you.

For example, I recall one day stepping out of my truck onto the site where I was developing and building a condominium project. It was a particularly difficult time immediately following the "9/11" terrorist attack in New York. It seemed likely that I would be financially wiped out and left responsible for huge loans I could never repay. I was discouraged and experiencing considerable fear. I was confident the Lord had led me into this business and now into this particular project. Furthermore, it seemed evident He had provided means for financing so I could accomplish it. Then, when the incredible pressure came and all seemed dismal, my decisions were challenged by the circumstances.

...when the atmosphere is healthy, the workers enjoy their work and know their good work will be financially rewarded.

That day, as I stepped out of my little white truck wearing my steel toed shoes and well-worn work clothes, I looked around at the fellas digging trenches with equipment, plumbers installing underground plumbing for a building and different kinds of activity all over the five acre work site. There were perhaps fifty men working there and few knew I was the reason they would have a paycheck that week. Most of them worked for one of my sub-contractors, not directly for me. As I was standing there, I was both admiring, hopeful and afraid. One of the workers who knew me came up to me and said, "Mr. Nelson, that guy way over there wants to know who you are. He said whoever you are he "wants to go to church wherever you do".

Surprised? Yes, I certainly was, and also immensely thankful. Why, at that moment, would a worker I didn't know have such an immediate impression about me like that? The only thing that came to mind was the scripture in Ecclesiastes 3:14, "I know that, whatsoever God doeth, it shall be for ever: nothing can be put to it, nor any thing taken from it: and God doeth it, that men should fear before Him."

At the moment, I felt like a basket case; but apparently the imprint of the Lord's work on me through the challenges and blessings of the years was more noticeable in my countenance than were the secret fears in my heart.

His eternal work would not be swayed by temporary situations. My trust in Him was not disappointed. Although current circumstances weighed on me like a ton of steel, what the Lord had engraved on me through the years seemed more evident to one of my workers than did the fleeting difficulties. Isn't God good? When God does something His way, it is quite impossible to be proud; but such a blessing caused me to be thankful.

I repeatedly heard from condominium buyers and workers that the atmosphere on this project was like no other they had ever seen. The workers were pleasant and glad to be there and the quality of work was superior to what was typical in the business. It confirmed to me again that when the atmosphere is healthy, the workers enjoy their work and know their good work will be financially rewarded.

As my son-in-law, Randy Sanders, explained to me, "If you don't have leadership, you have nothing. Your people will define your reputation. No matter who you work for, you are the commodity. (So), create a culture for others that you yourself would want to work in...".

"If you don't have leadership, you have nothing. Your people will define your reputation. (So), create a culture for others that you yourself would want to work in...".

-Randy Sanders

10. Respect: Who needs it?

How you treat people will affect how they respond to you. Your dress, the quality of your tools or book cases in the office, the quality of your vehicle and how organized you are...these and so many other things establish a statement about you to the observing world. Such things are superficial, but not unimportant. However, there is something deeper that precedes these things in significance.

So, before discussing these and other things, I wish to talk about my own attitude as "the boss". I noticed that there are particularly three things that are part of my job as a manager or as a business owner. With responsibility and accountability comes the third thing, authority. More than anything else, how I see my authority will most directly affect my relationship with my workers and those around me.

Responsibility. Accountability. Authority.

These three are like a three-legged stool. If one leg is broken, the stool will fall down. If they are all in good balance, the stool will hold a lot of weight for others to rest upon.

How I use my authority says much about my actual feelings about others. I can either use my authority to demonstrate my respect for them, or I can behave in a way to cause them to feel minimized and resentful. On the contrary, if I realize I am the first one that needs a great attitude and a serving heart, my helpers will know I respect them deeply, not just for what they can do for me, but just for whom they are. In turn, their respect for me will grow and the mutual appreciation we all have for each other will create a great atmosphere.

Responsibility. Accountability. Authority. These three are like a three-legged stool. If one leg is broken, the stool will fall down. If they are all in good balance, the stool will hold a lot of weight for others to rest upon. I must be responsible, I must be accountable and I must use the built-in authority with honor.

While responsibility and accountability are major issues, they are not so personal as authority. They affect the business in other ways, but how I treat others as their boss affects the very people who are helpful to me so my business can succeed. I ought not express my authority as though parading with self-importance. I ought not try to impress others with how powerful I am. If I have authority, I need to use it to lift them up where they are and make them happy to be alive and happy to be on the job with me. This will inspire them to do their best and there will be no lack of respect in any direction.

Whether on the job or at home, this should be my opportunity to bless others with my understanding and attitude about this "three-legged stool". In dealing with legal issues and city hall and banks and others, I need to be responsible and accountable. But, perhaps most of all, I need to learn to be respectful of those who work with me and for me. I may expect them to work well with a great attitude, but I need to be the first one to demonstrate such a disposition. I hire them as helpers, as workers, as sub-contractors.

They are not my servants, they are my helpers. If there is a servant attitude to be had, it should start with me.

While I realize I could squeeze a lot out of them beyond their responsibility by using my authority over them, that is not right. They are not my servants, they are my helpers. If there is a servant attitude to be had, it should start with me. I did, in fact, notice that as the authority that came with my position grew, I delighted to *use it to serve others, not beat them into submission* so I might look like "a tough guy". My desire to be a servant boss is not a matter of *weakness*! No! It is a matter of *meekness*.

In other words, the best way for me to learn how to be "over" others is for my heart to freshly seek to be "under" God. There I find perspective of who I am and where I am. There I touch the love and energy of God that strengthens me and delights to serve and lead others—His way—wisely, humbly, meekly, firmly and rightly.

Remember Moses? He was considered by God as being meek more than any man on the face of the earth. (Numbers 12:3). So then, Moses was *meek*? Now, would you say that Moses was *weak*? I think not- quite the opposite in fact! When he and Aaron were "in Pharaoh's face" with promises of plagues and the death of Pharaoh's son, do you think Pharaoh considered Moses weak? How about when Moses stepped into the Red Sea, making a sidewalk for the Israelites and a grave for the Egyptians? Was Moses weak then? Far from it! Yet, he remained meek, a powerful statement in itself of security in God and a servant's heart to his people.

If we have authority over others in management or as an employer, may we understand the great importance of this kind of thinking. To be a "Christian boss" is to be meek, not weak. With such an attitude, honor comes to us from grateful people. Honor grows of its own accord, it can never be required. If a boss has a servant's respectful demeanor, respect shown by his workers and associates is spontaneous and lasting. Relationships will flourish, people will respond and the business will grow. That should not be the motive, but it will likely be the result!

In moments, I can realize the value of a man and his work by his attitude and how he handles things.

Honor grows of its own accord, it can never be required.

Now, a few words about workers on the job and what their demeanor seemed to say about respect. As a general contractor on a project, I often saw a tradesman drive in and inquire about work. If his pickup was all beat up on the outside and sloppy on the inside, I knew immediately something important about him. Inevitably, such a person had a low value of his worth. He would typically offer to work for low wages and his quality of work was often poor.

Others were impressive by how their vehicle appeared, the condition of their tires, the condition and arrangement of their tools in the truck and how they appeared personally. I can usually tell immediately how a man will do on the job by the way he gets out of his truck, the look on his face, if he is on time or late, how he treats the tool in his hand and what quality of tool he buys, how he greets his co-workers, etc. If I watch him work and *how* he works for five minutes I know exactly who I have at hand and what I can likely expect from him.

In his mind, a worker may think his value is about the time he puts in. In moments, I can realize the value of a man and his work by his attitude and how he handles things. It is not a matter of time he "puts in" but of his production and the attitude and quality with which it is done. If he doesn't respect his pliers or electric drill, or the books in his office or the laptop on his desk, I know something about his thinking. His countenance betrays his deeper thought and the respect or disrespect that is reflected by his attitude and appearance says more than a framed degree on his wall could ever tell me. If a man doesn't respect himself, there is no reason to expect he will respect me or his fellow workers, his tools or the project that will affect my reputation.

Even a tradesman doing the roughest work can create his own great atmosphere. A roofer climbing a ladder or a plumber crawling under a house may have torn clothes and grease on his hands, but his sober attitude and personable countenance explain all that other workers and the boss need to know about him. A polished professional in the office may hide his arrogant or troubled self under a little more culture, but who he is will always be defined by his attitude, by what he does and by how he does it. Whether for better or for worse, in a man's work and presence there will be a flavor, an atmosphere either of distance or of attractiveness that he creates around him. There tends to be a clear indication of how the person thinks and works.

At the end of the day, a person must be worthy of his hire by what kind of a person he is and how he does his job.

Through trying to help careless and sloppy people do better and being intimidated by those who looked like they were doing well, I learned an important lesson. I realized I lost income on some workers who were pleased with a minimum wage. In other cases, I prospered with some workers whom I paid twice as much as the market would suggest.

I quickly learned that our "time" is worth nothing. Punching a clock may be necessary, but a person's measureable value is not in the hours he spends but what he accomplishes during the time on the clock. What is measureable is not the time but what a man does with his time. Whether on salary, on piece-work contracts or hourly wage, it all comes down to producing a product or providing a service of some sort.

What you provide may be a physical item in a factory or construction site; or it may be the students at a private school or a couple being counseled in their marriage.

At the end of the day, a person must be worthy of his hire by what kind of a person he is and how he does his job.

A person who will not improve and has no heart to learn new things and better ways will tend to suffer forever. Why? Because such a person is inclined to explain away his laziness, or his inferiority of preparation, or his resentment of responsibility by complaining that "the rich take all the good jobs". With such a person there is no respect either received or given. As believers, we may learn the depths of what happens to our heart and mind and character when the importance of being respectful and becoming respectable touches the deepest part of our personality.

The person who uses his time properly will always be in the "driver's seat" because he has learned to respect himself, serve others, and know the value of a job properly and thoroughly well done.

The person who uses his time properly will always be in the "driver's seat" because he has learned to respect himself, serve others, and know the value of a job properly and thoroughly well done. Such a person need not drop by a project or store to "see if they are hiring".

I submit to you the thought that everyone is hiring. If you can demonstrate you are needed and that you will be of both personal and financial value to a client or to a company, you become the one in the "driver's seat". You can create your own pocket of value for someone else or extend it to your own business in self-employment. Don't be the one who complains no one is hiring. Be the innovator who creates a market and become the one who hires. Then you will know the excitement and the value of being self-employed.

I learned to understand the importance of simple respect in daily life on the job. As a Christian I understood the idea, but it tested me much to see how it could work out in my life at work. By unusual circumstances, I somehow qualified to apply for a license as a General Contractor in Denver in 1973 and was shocked to discover I passed the examination the first time.

Not long before, I was teaching junior high school in the ghettoes of Los Angeles. I became extremely ill and had to give up my job. After about fifteen months I had enough strength to do some small handyman jobs, yet after two years I was still very weak. I had almost no tools or interest or capabilities in construction. My natural gifts and desires were not in such things at all.

Suddenly, I was the president of an incorporated construction business with two other friends in Colorado. Chuck knew something about how to keep accounting books and Ron had a small amount of experience as a carpenter. I had little knowledge of either one, but I liked people, liked to study and was the one who qualified for the public examination.

With such beggarly experience, our union corporation somehow was awarded the contract to build a Sizzler Steak House. We were hired by Walt, an aging superintendent who worked for a California company. He said he wanted us to work with him because he "liked us" and he just "knew" he could trust us.

We had no clue of how to bid the job or even do the work, but he told us what the company paid the builder on their last project, and that the job was ours if we wanted it. Being inexperienced and new in the field, we had need of certain equipment to do such a huge project.

Walt volunteered to let us use some of his tools. Why? He said, "because I see how you fellas take care of your tools, so I know you will take care of mine". This beginning of significant projects was based more on respect than on skill. In due time, as respect was our way of life, the skills came, and with that came a growing, profitable and respectable business.

In due time, as respect was our way of life, the skills came, and with that came a growing, profitable and respectable business.

11. Legal issues (1)

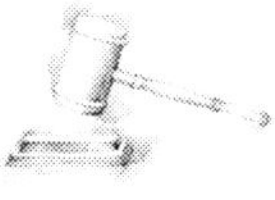

Sooner or later, you will face legal trouble as you are exposed to the public in your business. Many Christians are uncomfortable in dealing with legal issues. Many such conflicts in a believer may arise from his own uncertainty about biblical relationships and biblical perspective in them. In the next section we will discuss and expand these considerations further, due to the importance of relationship and testimony between believers and the testimony of the believers in the church and of the church in the community. You will need to settle it in your own heart before you get involved in business what you will do with such things.

You will perhaps have questions such as:

1. "What if a customer doesn't pay me and I find out he is a Christian? The Bible says to not take a brother to court. What should I do?"

2. "What if a worker steals from me or damages my reputation in my business? The Bible says to "turn the other cheek". What should I do?"

What if a worker steals from me or damages my reputation in my business? The Bible says to "turn the other cheek". What should I do?

3. "What if I lose a contract or promotion because someone lied about me or was dishonest in the way they advanced themselves and undermined me? Shouldn't a Christian be humble and meek and not defend himself?"

4. "What if a government agency or worker's compensation fund damages me financially through dishonesty or obvious abuse? Isn't every government from God? As a Christian shouldn't I be passive and let whatever happens to me be God's responsibility instead of mine? If God doesn't protect me in evil situations such as this, does this mean I'm suffering for the sake of His kingdom and I will receive eternal reward later (even if it means I go bankrupt now and can't provide for my family any more)? Doesn't the Bible say, 'Vengeance is mine, I will repay', says the Lord? Do these thoughts apply to my business?"

5. "What if a Christian "brother" makes me sign a contract of what I will do for him but then later won't pay me when I'm done "because he doesn't feel led of the Lord" to pay me right now?"

6. "What if I preach to one of my employees or customers on the job and then they turn against me and won't work well or won't pay for my services because they consider me a hypocrite?"

These problems, and many others, will likely come your way, especially if you don't understand who you are, what it means to be a Christian and why you are in business. To some, these six problems might seem absurd, but others know that problems like this are real and painful and paralyzing. The more a believer is sincere, the more likely he is to have serious problems like this. Because he is sincere, he may be inclined to get God's economy and the material economy all tangled up and confused with each other. As a result, what should be pretty simple may become extremely painful, complicated and a defeat in both business and personal life.

I will not try to answer these questions for you. These are only a few of many questions and many situations that may come your way. Sometimes there may be more than one answer in a situation, depending on the persons and circumstances involved. Sometimes there is no "right" or "wrong" answer, but just a "gray area" allowing for personal convictions and personal opinions before the Lord.

Mostly, these type of questions should cause you to seek wisdom of the Lord in the Word of the Lord. Remember, God is personal, He is not a religion. Talk to Him and seek His impression in you when things are not so clear. Fellowship with other spiritual and practical believers who have already experienced such challenges in their businesses.

Remember, God is personal, He is not a religion. Talk to Him and seek His impression in you when things are not so clear.

12. Legal issues (2)

Some Christians really get tangled up in this matter of *how* to be a Christian, *how* to do business properly and *if* there is a conflict between the two. Suppose you have signed a contract with someone and then he decides not to pay you. If you find out "he is a Christian brother" should you hold him accountable in court?

What I will share with you now may be difficult for some to hear. Thoughts about this topic in the way I present it are personal and sensitive, so I share my opinion only. What is the comfort and peace in my conscience may be different than what you find at this time in yours. Please read, knowing that your heart, your decisions and your viewpoint in the Lord's Word is for your own discretion and application. Regardless of your thoughts, I hope you will be helped by mine.

Perhaps you will face situations such as the following:

1. Let me ask you something. Are you in business or are you starting a ministry or mission project?

Are you operating a Mission or a Business? Is there a difference to you?

2. If you are in business, you sign contracts. If you don't, you are trusting in a humanity that is fallen, regardless who the person is. I once did repeatedly large projects for a hateful man who had a reputation for destroying others. When I asked him to sign my contract, he got angry and said "Contracts are for crooks!", but he signed anyway. Eventually, he liked me a lot and obviously knew I was a person he could fully trust. Clearly, he had never known anyone else like me.

By and by, I let my weaker, trusting side prevail and did a large project without a signed contract because I just "knew" by that time I could trust him. I learned painfully that he was right. "Contracts are for crooks" and he proved he was the crook that everyone else in the metropolitan business community knew he was. He knew he was a crook and it just took awhile for me to believe it and suffer the consequences for it.

He eventually trusted me so much that he asked my wife and me to give him and his wife marriage counseling. We tried to help them. We also went beyond our business relationship by wanting to help them find Christ. It was not too much later when he set out to rob me, so what next? What would you do? Would you let your family suffer under a loss of several hundred thousand dollars and a personal agony that lasted years, or would you bring legal pressure to bear upon him?

3. If you sign a contract, do you ask a customer if he is a Christian? If so, and he is, do you let him know you don't expect him to pay you "unless he feels led of the

Lord to do so"? If that is how you do business, why would you ask him to sign a document in the beginning anyway? This may sound ridiculous, but for some it is not.

4. If you sign a contract which indicates your responsibility and the responsibility also of your customer, that is a legal issue. Why would you have difficulty, then, of pressing the customer legally to pay for what he legally agreed to? Will he not press you legally to keep your commitment in the contract? Are you operating a Mission or a Business? Is there a difference to you?

5. If you try to adhere to I Corinthians 6:1-7, you would do well to consider the context and the church situation. Unlike the days of the original churches, the church today is divided into splinters of people who neither know each other nor have a testimony of Christ and the church in their community. This passage would seem to assume that the brothers are in the church together and are both under the authority of church government. If they choose the world's court system in place of that, such activity is a shame to the church and its testimony.

What about today? The Bible is still the Bible and the truth is unchanged. What has changed? Neither the truth nor the hope, but the circumstance. If my customer is a Christian but not subject to the same church government I have, there is no leverage and perhaps no public testimony to maintain. If we both used a legal contract of the world's designation, I hurt only myself, my reputation, my family and my ability to provide for my family by letting evil have its way.

I respect others and I keep the law but I wisely live so my customers know I expect no less from them.

I do not encourage you to resort to worldly law easily. On the other hand, being in business is an exercise of employment in that arena. I do well to be wise enough to live carefully and give the benefit to a slacker, but I also do well to let people realize I know how to do business properly. I am meek but I am not weak. I am humble but I am not a rug to be walked upon. I respect others and I keep the law but I wisely live so my customers know I expect no less from them. Out of this understanding comes mutual respect, and happily, the problems thereafter are few.

13. Government issues and requirements

The believer is a citizen of two worlds. It takes much wisdom, much insight and careful practice in learning how to dwell properly in the two worlds simultaneously. For the Christian, his heart and purpose and future is eternal. Each day is about the life of eternity being worked out in the here and now. How to maintain such a heavenly view in an earthly situation is challenging. I welcome the challenge, for it is in this way I have begun learning to know Christ in a practical application that not only provides for my family, but affects the business and neighborhood and church community wherever I am.

I suggest a few of many possible thoughts regarding government issues:

If I choose to do business on "the world's playing field", I need to keep the rules they provide "or there is no need to show up for the game".

1. A legitimate business requires a legitimate status. A believer's view of government can really help him or really hinder him in doing business. Some believers make it their mission to fight the corruption in government. They tend to get in trouble because of their views about paying taxes and licenses and keeping local codes. As for me, I prefer to submit to government requirements and save my energy and time for being productive in my business, in my family life and in my church life.

There is a war we need to fight, but for me, it is not primarily the dishonesty and usury of government. If I choose to do business on "the world's playing field", I need to keep the rules they provide "or there is no need to show up for the game". You may like European soccer, but if you insist on playing by the rules of American football, you will indeed fight a battle, but a foolish one. I found the same principle is true in doing business.

2. Not every government regulation makes sense. Just as it may not make sense to go 15 mph through a school zone on Saturday afternoon when the yellow flashing light was left on by mistake, so it is with many, many codes and regulations. Ignore them or pay the price at your own discretion.

When I first started Morning Star Construction Co. in Denver in 1973, I had no business experience, no training in business and no previous ambition to be in business. I also had no money. To pay the rent of $150 per month on the well-used house on South Wolf Street was a real stretch of my capability. Suddenly, I was a licensed contractor with large and impressive contracts awarded to me.

One of the first things I tried to avoid was paying a premium for Workers Compensation Insurance. It was expensive and to me it seemed a meaningless waste of money. My employees were nearly all believers who would probably not betray me if they had a small injury and everyone that worked for me seemed to be careful, anyway. The idea of "wasting" money I didn't have on something that didn't seem to matter fell into the category of "The Ridiculous", as far as I was concerned.

I recall wrestling with this idea and then I remembered how my dad had told me it was always a good idea to obey the law. Stretching out really far, with Dad's advice in my mind, I bought a policy and resented it every day afterward, although it somehow made me feel good to have it.

I recall wrestling with this idea and then I remembered how my dad had told me it was always a good idea to obey the law.

Then, one day, everything changed. One of my workers was of retirement age and was working with his son for me on a high scaffold. As they were installing siding on a two story townhouse, the scaffold plank they were standing on snapped in half. They fell about twenty feet to the hard, uneven ground.

Mr. Davis broke his back and he was never able to work again. That day, I was sorry for him and what had happened, but I was thankful he would be cared for as long as necessary. A further bonus was that I would not lose my contractor's license or spend the rest of my life caring for my worker and his family when I could barely provide for my own. I was indeed thankful Dad had taught me to obey the law.

3. When you are self-employed, you no longer have a superior doing all the paperwork for you. Suddenly, there are mountains of paper requirements by various agencies that you must address, whether you know it or not, and whether you like it or not. It is up to you to take the initiative to see what the governments on every level expect from you. It is important you find an informed accountant who can advise you of your exposure to government requirements. Ask around for a good referral. Like anything else, there are good ones and bad ones, those who care and those who don't, those who are fair and those who take advantage.

...you simply cannot afford to try and save money by exercising your ignorance and hoping nobody notices.

The same goes for finding an attorney to be on hand for legal counsel of various kinds, not just if or when you get sued. Use them for your informed advantage, don't let them use you for their piggybank. Ask many questions until you actually understand things. Remember, you are the boss. Do not be intimidated by their thick carpet and flashy clothes. They work for you and they will do best when you behave yourself in a way they realize you know that.

Even when short on money, I found it a good investment to let my accountant handle all my quarterly and annual forms for the various required taxes and also calculate and submit for me my annual IRS tax return reports. This is one area where you simply cannot afford to try and save money by exercising your ignorance and hoping nobody notices. Use your time to do the things you do best that bring income to your business. Hire others to do what they do best if that means you can do more of what you do better.

Use your time to do the things you do best that bring income to your business. Hire others to do what they do best if that means you can do more of what you do better.

One of these responsibilities is paying your own taxes. You need to lay aside your taxes as you go, preferably in an interest-bearing, money market fund with check-writing capability. Do not dream you can do it later. If you can not keep up now, how can you catch up later? Do not make your mission in life as a self-employed person to defy the government and its tactics about using your hard-earned money for political purposes. You have a war to fight- deceiving the government and avoiding taxes should not be it. If you think that is your war, you might want to re-consider your intention of being self-employed and providing for your family by this means.

Take time to calculate how much money you need to set aside for taxes every week or month. As far as the government is concerned, *this is not your money anyway, so don't dream you can use it temporarily and not have a problem finding an adequate amount to pay your taxes when they come due.* Set aside more than you need to, in case you are in error. If you saved too much, a tax rebate is better than a payment deficit.

Develop your personal budget around the remaining figure. Taxes, off the top. Tithes and gifts to the Lord's work, off the top (Which top? Your gross earnings or your earnings after taxes? You need to ask the Lord and be at peace with Him and with your spouse).

Now, figure out the budget by which you can provide for your family. This manner will make the government happy and the Lord's blessing will always be with you. The government's trust is in you. Your trust must be in God. Then, you and your family and the church will all be blessed in the peace of Christ.

The government's trust is in you. Your trust must be in God. Then, you and your family and the church will all be blessed in the peace of Christ.

4. Depending on where you live and your local regulation, there are numerous legal things you need to know about. Do not assume your ignorance about government is ok or that it will excuse you. It is not ok and it will not excuse you if you break the law. Do not assume "everything will work out ok". It may, but it usually does not. Be proactive and prepared or wait to be reactive and punished. If you drive "50 mph" in a "35 mph" zone, it does not matter if you have overlooked the sign. The policeman will write a ticket because you broke the law and he likely will not excuse you just because you appear to be a nice person. The same principle applies to business requirements in government.

By the way, you can learn what kind of things you need to know by being thorough in all you do. Don't just make a telephone call about something and ask one question. Ask a lot of questions from whoever you talk to about your job interests. If you go to City Hall, ask what you know you should ask, then ask them what questions you should be asking that you don't know about.

Be proactive and prepared or wait to be reactive and punished.

If you go to a library, look up literature that may be helpful, then ask the librarian what other resources and questions and people you should talk to about your job situation. If you find someone who has experienced self-employment, don't settle for a casual question or two. Ask them if they would invest some time in helping you know what to do so you can get a great start and learn how to be the best in whatever you do. By the way, experienced people often take delight in sharing with eager younger ones what they have learned.

Ask the Lord to give you a spiritual and practical mentor.

Pray much, study much, read Proverbs and other scriptures a lot. Ask the Lord to give you a spiritual and practical mentor. As an extension of that, fellowship with older and wiser men in the faith, and observe those who have done well in worldly wisdom and with their ventures into business. These resources will help you in legal understanding, but they will be helpful in so much more. Take the time to develop a relationship with several people who can really be helpful to you. They will feel esteemed that you desire their opinion and fellowship. Ask them to pray with you and for you. Ask them to mentor you and to be hard on you in accounting to them for practical matters. You will honor them much by your interest and your reciprocation of kindness and care.

As to responsibilities once you are in the business mode, you will have many things to know and do related to government. In my business exposure through the years, I have paid state taxes, local taxes, federal taxes, business license requirements, workers compensation requirements, health insurance deductions for employees, social security deductions, unemployment insurance deductions, local and state contractor license tests and certifications and scheduled renewals, required ongoing education units, and so forth.

One annual business tax where I live is called a personalty tax. (This is not a typo for "personality"; it is an annual assessment on everything I use in business). If I bought a tool or a desk for my office or any other such thing, I pay a tax every year on the same item. If I wasted money and was not responsible, this is not a problem to the tax authorities; but if I sacrificed and improved my equipment instead of wasting the money on pleasures of some sort, I pay a personalty tax on it. This tax may feel like a punishment for being responsible enough and sacrificial enough to have grown a business others want to imitate or work for. Pay it? Yes, that's the law. Deal with it or don't go into business.

Paying the tax(es) is not optional. Paying them late usually brings late fees and compounding interest. Not paying them at all can lead to further complications. If you are in business, this is part of your price tag. If you don't prepare yourself for this part of your public responsibility it can be a serious blow to your long term stability and financial health. This is not something you fight. This is something you plan for and include in your business budget and schedule.

Even if you believe it is against the U.S. Constitution for the government to force you to pay taxes and perform legal endeavors, it will be a sapping of your energy and purpose and finances to refuse to cooperate. If you choose to be in business, you have chosen to "play on that field". Either play it well and honestly or work for someone else who will play it for you and pay you less.

If you choose to be in business, you have chosen to "play on that field". Either play it well and honestly or work for someone else who will play it for you and pay you less.

As a Christian, I have learned my primary job is to live Christ in integrity that I might provide for my family's needs. My passion is with a heavenly mind but my hands need to work righteously on the earth. Being taxed on nearly every aspect of business is "one of the little troublesome mosquitoes" that make the journey exciting and memorable.

14. Business financing for the self-employed

This point is especially for the self-employed. I have always heard that small businesses are the back-bone of America. While that is likely accurate, those who are self-employed may soon feel like the financial and legislative world is trying to break their back of any bone it still has.

I have had countless experiences along the way that made this evident to me. Just one of them may make the point. It is about my effort to get a loan to work on our house.

Clients sometimes came to our home to see what quality of work they could expect from me on their construction project. It was always easier to show someone what I have actually done than to convince them what I thought I could do for them. With this in mind, I wanted to complete the extensive project at home that we had been working on for a very long time. The need was apparent and it seemed like the time had finally come when I could spend some time and finish the job.

This matter was not simple and gaining financing was challenging. You may wonder what our situation was at the time, so I would like to share a little of it with you. I had just finished commuting more than 2000 miles for over three years to save my family and our house and general situation from total financial and functional loss. To address the need and recover from excruciating financial and personal pressures realized in business, most years I could visit home for only 8-10 weekends a year.

He liked me and my work and workers so much he didn't want me to have any other clients. He wanted to "own" me even though I had other contracts and ongoing commitments.

As you might imagine, it was an extremely challenging time for me and for my wife and four teenage children. This particular situation developed when one of my clients became jealous of me and told me he wanted me all to himself. He liked me and my work and workers so much he didn't want me to have any other clients. He wanted to "own" me even though I had other contracts and ongoing commitments. When that was not agreeable with me, he said he was determined to destroy me and my business. I had watched him do this to others and he wasted no time in his evil attacks on me. I had to take work out of state to recover from the resulting devastation.

When I was at last able to come home to stay, I was still under much financial stress, but at least able to care for my family better. Our place was large and I had done much to improve it, but it still needed about $30,000 to finish what I had begun. Once the house would be presentable, I planned to sell it and break free of the endless, crushing debts that had come upon me due to my former client's antics.

Before I had to leave home and commute those three years and four months, I had enlarged the heated space of our house to about 6900 square feet and it was setting on seventeen acres in the city limits. I had built a 2300 square foot, rather exotic deck, which people admired very much. I applied for a loan and paid the bank for an appraisal to establish the current house value.

When the appraiser came, he refused to count the number of bathrooms or bedrooms correctly, and reported other things inaccurately as well. The appraisal came back much less than expected. I went to the bank, where I had been a dependable and responsible customer for more than seven years. Unlike ever before, the manager was rude, spoke angrily to me and refused to discuss the appraisal, which was obviously in extreme error.

Sometime later, I was standing on the deck with my loan officer, further exploring with him the status of the loan application. He was obviously greatly impressed with our house and acknowledged the importance of finishing the remaining package of items I proposed. To get the equity loan did not seem to me like it should be difficult, since we still showed about 50% equity in spite of the low appraisal. During that period of time, any person, even without a job, could qualify for a loan with such equity. I was aware some lenders made loans to high equity situations and even hoped the homeowner would fail later so they could repossess the house and sell it for a big profit. I also learned the bank considered me a reliable person and a businessman with "golden credit". Furthermore, I had never been sued by any customer during over 500 jobs in my years in the construction business, which is nearly unheard of. I had never been bankrupt, failed in legal or financial responsibilities and had the finest reputation. This should be good enough to get a small loan, right?

Near the end of our "interview" while standing on the deck, I asked him, "Well, can you make the loan to me?"

"No, I can't", he said.

Astonished, I asked, "Why?"

"Because you are self-employed and you have to prove yourself", he said.

The bank considered me a reliable person and a businessman with "golden credit". Near the end of our "interview" while standing on the deck, I asked him, "Well, can you make the loan to me?" "No, I can't", he said... "because you are self-employed..."

"Well, I have been self-employed with a successful business for over fifteen years. How long does it take before I have an adequate track record?"

He couldn't answer that, but said that since I was self-employed I was too risky for the bank. I then said, "Let me ask you something. Suppose a carpenter employee of mine comes to you for a loan to buy a house. Suppose you learn he has been employed two years by my company, has good credit and seems like a reliable person. Will you give him a loan?"

Without hesitation, the bank officer said "Of course!"

"Why?", I asked.

"Because he has a job", he said.

With a proper attitude, I continued, "Let me ask you something further. Did it ever occur to you that if business got slow and there was enough work for only one person I would have to fire all my workers? If I did that, would I not have a job? Would I not be the only one working and I would be making all the money for myself? All of my former workers would be unemployed, including the one you approved for a loan, and I would be the only one with an income. Does this make a difference to you?"

He seemed absolutely amazed at my logic and question. "Why, I never even thought of that!", he said, with a bright light in his eyes and countenance.

It was obvious he liked me, was pleased with me personally and impressed with my situation and track record. I was relieved that I had surely made my point.

"So then", I said, "do I get the loan?"

With a suddenly sour look on his face again, he

said, "No, you don't!"

"Why not?", I asked.

"Because you are self-employed!"

The interview was over and it seemed for awhile like an important part of my life was too.

Lest you think there is no hope for good things in self-employment, I must add something and tell you otherwise. Actually, there is great opportunity, much experience and much benefit in such a work profile. As time and experience went on, I gained much favor with lenders and building departments wherever I worked. Eventually, I grew accustomed to having a bank manager call me and ask if the bank could loan me some money for anything. I do admit that it felt really good to turn them down the first time and tell them I didn't need them at the moment.

Of course, the relationship(s) were nurtured with great trust and good experience on both sides. The lenders became excellent resources for me of both financing and evaluating the likely success of my projects. In one of my last developments, it was a delight to me that both my banker and my potential customers got "mad" at me only one time. The bank was upset because I had sold my last condominium in the project. They liked to work with me and they liked the way I did things. The potential customers were upset because all my units were sold on that project and there were not any they could buy.

No matter what the challenges are, once you are self-employed it seems almost unthinkable to work on someone else's 9-5 clock again.

As challenging as working for yourself is, there is something about it that is special. The flexibility and opportunities that come with it can, and should be, worth what you lose being on the clock and rigid schedule of another company that gains the profits of your hard work, commitment, talent and imagination. No matter what the challenges are, once you are self-employed it seems almost unthinkable to work on someone else's 9-5 clock again.

Still, whatever your job or profession is, hard times or boring days seem to bring fantasies of greener pastures. I was once in a meeting in which a Christian brother testified about his job. He is a PhD in chemistry and has a wonderful situation. He said that sometimes he just sits at his company desk and dreams of being self-employed. I knew I had to respond. I took the chance to share my experience of having my own company. I said that sometimes I just dream of the luxury of working for someone else again and get all the benefit that comes with that situation.

What is the bottom line? Whatever we do, we must be at peace with the Lord and be always under His leading and care.

15. Business model(s)

So, you are going to work for yourself? No matter what you do in self-employment, you will need to do a certain amount of paperwork. Before getting too involved with accountants or attorneys, you may spend some time looking at a major office supply store. You can buy complex forms for nearly any business model inexpensively.

If you spend some time this way to understand what is involved in your state and in your city, you can save a lot of money while getting started properly and meeting legal expectations. Do not assume you can do whatever you want and the government won't notice or care. Those who have such a careless attitude inevitably suffer. Those who "play" carelessly will "pay" heavily.

Do not assume you can do whatever you want and the government won't notice or care. Those who have such a careless attitude inevitably suffer.

Let me share a few suggestions:

1. Inquire of a bookkeeper, godly experienced business people, and an accountant or an attorney as to what business model will best fit your intentions. Many cities and towns have meetings just for Christians who own businesses of a great variety. They come together regularly to pray and fellowship together and learn from each other many relevant things. You may inquire of church leadership and civic leaders whether there is such a group. If there is not, perhaps you can begin one.

2. Sole proprietor? In this case you work only for yourself without employees. This is by far the simplest, and a good way to start while you consider how it will be "working for yourself". If you are employed elsewhere, you might start something on the side and let it build up into a full time business. At such a time, you could always consider another business model.

3. Business partners with your spouse? On occasion, this is workable. For most people, it is "too much of a good thing". Unless your marriage is fine-tuned and can handle unspeakable additional stresses from the business world, it will be a great problem to your family life, if not sooner, then later. If you can handle this kind of complicated addition to your marriage, make certain both of you are in tune with the Lord, with each other, and under a clear, encouraging, confirming fellowship with people who love you and have your best interests in mind. Discuss in advance what responsibilities, time commitments and schedules will be involved for your spouse. Be proactive thoughtfully or your marriage and business will suffer re-actively and painfully.

As challenging as working for yourself is, there is something about it that is special…. the flexibility and opportunities that come with it.

4. Partnership? Occasionally, but very rarely, have I ever seen a partnership work well. No matter how much you trust your friend and no matter how much you have in common, partnerships are extremely difficult. Parting ways later inevitably is a stress on what used to be a good friendship or fellowship with that brother or sister in the church. Marriage is hard enough. At least when you are married, you can "kiss and make up" when solving a problem. It doesn't work like that in business!

5. Corporation? What kind of corporation? LLC? This choice depends on numerous things. Although you can get inexpensive forms to fill out and file them yourself in your state, corporations are complicated, time consuming, and not always beneficial to tax savings. Even protection from creditors and imposing people is not always a certainty. With so many rules and guidelines to follow, even one mistake in your corporate history will allow your protective covering to be pierced by someone who wants to sue you, whether there is grounds for a lawsuit or not. Legal counsel may advise you to do what is good for their high fees, not what will meet your need, so be mindful of that. Nevertheless, before you make a decision about incorporating, this is one place where legal counsel from an attorney and an accountant is worthwhile.

Study this situation carefully, inquire much of others before making this big decision. Don't be afraid of it. At the same time, don't stumble into it blindly on casual advice or passive assumptions.

6. As for me, I have tried different business models along the way. I have had a sole proprietorship, a corporation and some partnerships. For the most part, I preferred the simple proprietorship model, even when I lately did over $5,000,000 of construction business in a year. I had no secretary, no foreman, no superintendent, no employees, no accountant or attorney on retainer or payroll.

I made every agreement with every worker and reviewed every invoice. My wife learned to pay invoices for me, helped with some filing and often helped clean my houses or condominiums or room additions. I subcontracted everything, supervised everything myself and worked on the jobsites with my hands alongside my helpers as much as possible. I hired short term help as needed and my accountant on occasion through the year for basic updates for lenders, government forms and IRS returns.

By the time I learned to do this kind of volume in this way, I had much extra time. Most weeks I could spend many hours writing and publishing, serving others and spending 20-40 hours in church ministry and leadership.

Sole proprietor? Partnership?
Corporation?
Which business model is best?

16. Scheduling your day and your life

Scheduling.

"Scheduling! Did you say scheduling? What would I schedule? When I need something done I do it and I finish it when I have time. Besides, I don't have that many things to keep track of!"

"Scheduling! Did you say scheduling? What would I schedule?"

If this is your response, you are a typical person. Still, you are not completely typical because you have the desire to improve your situation by starting your own business or moving up into higher management where you work. In this matter I am strongly opinionated. Let me tell you clearly that it is really important to plan and schedule how you will spend your day, your month, your year and your life. The American culture doesn't teach us this, schools don't teach us this and churches don't teach or preach this.

Nevertheless, I submit it is something we all would do well to learn. The sooner we start, the better. Buy a pocket calendar. If you can only think of one thing to write down this week, do it. Once you begin, you may find you need to write smaller to make room on the provided area.

Appointment with a client. He cancels, so reschedule and write it down and be there five minutes early. Call to schedule your vehicle service and write it down. Save time by scheduling instead of just showing up and waiting or being rejected. Get the name of the service personnel, be five minutes early and ask for him or her. Shake hands firmly and look them in the eye. Ask for the information you need before committing to it. If you don't have the work done then, write down the day and time to return.

Let me tell you clearly that it is really important to plan and schedule how you will spend your day, your month, your year and your life.

What about your stops on the way home? Who will take care of these things, or do they "just happen" or do you get home and find out you have to go back out to do some things because you didn't schedule it with your spouse or child or? So you use extra gas, you don't get your work done and make less money because of it. You get frustrated with yourself or your spouse and you have to explain to your client why you forgot to call him back or deliver what he ordered from you...Why didn't you schedule these things first thing this morning? You could have had peace instead of frustration, and satisfaction instead of a sense of waste.

Groceries, hardware tools. People you need to pray for and talk to about business or neighborly things today or next month. Write it down. If you don't get something done that day, forward it to the next day or the next week and write it down. When it is done, cross it off before starting the next day. Etc.

Your efforts and your needs will train you. If you can spend some time alone with the Lord in the morning, you will likely be able to think clearly after that and address priorities of the day. Write them down. Every day, including holidays.

Does this sound hard? Does an engine have a hard time running without oil? No doubt, your engine would have a hard time. Put some oil in the engine, lubricate it and let it run awhile. No problem. Likewise, let your life, your needs, your personal and family and church and business needs guide you, lubricate you, as to what to schedule. Write them down, prioritize them and make a plan for the day.

Time is not a renewable asset. When it is gone, you lie down and never get up again. So use your allotted time well, use it wisely, use it day by day with the Lord's leading and your discipline to schedule it.

Whew!! Are you exhausted yet? Only if you haven't found what a benefit this is and how easy it is. The more you exercise in it the more it is like you have "oiled your engine". Your life and your day gains perspective.

Things you do matter. You can go bankrupt and start over. You can break a valuable possession and someday by a new one. But...waste one minute and it is gone forever. The only possession you truly have is your time.

Time is not a renewable asset. When it is gone, you lie down and never get up again. So use your allotted time well, use it wisely, use it day by day with the Lord's leading and your discipline to schedule it.

You may still say this is good for some people, but not for you. Many Christians believe, as the Bible explains it in places such as Romans 1, that God has revealed himself in creation.

Let me ask you something. Do you believe this? If so, let me ask you something else. Have you noticed how in creation God scheduled the universe, the details of His creation in Genesis 1-2 and Job 38, the order in which He created things, the years, the four seasons, the seven days, the twenty four hours each day, the minutes, the seconds? Did you notice that the Bible even shows the Father has scheduled the exact moment of the return of Christ? "...for even the Son knows not when, but only the Father...so be ye always ready for in such an hour as ye think not He will come". Have you not read in The Revelation how He has things written down in His book of life?

Don't trust a great life with a limited mind. Write things down so you can be free to live.

If we would enter into the creative pattern and life of our Creator, I submit to you we would do well to learn to use our days wisely with Him as our source of inspiration and guidance. Don't trust a great life with a limited mind. Write things down so you can be free to live.

Ok, let's move on with a few more thoughts now. I once read a survey that attempted to identify common traits in "successful" people. While being a biblical Christian is hard to define in terms of "success", being in business and having responsibilities and relationships with others is not. The survey I read considered important things the persons might have in common, such as education, gender, race, religion, training, etc. As it turned out, the only thing every "successful" person had in common was a habit of "writing things down".

My own previous and continuing experience certainly affirms that conclusion to me. I have found nothing more helpful in planning and thinking clearly about time planning than using a pocket calendar with sections for daily, weekly, quarterly and annual scheduling.

This is not merely an act of writing something down. It is a way of thinking and our ways of thinking build our habits and habits are what compose our character.

This is not merely an act of writing something down. It is a way of thinking and our ways of thinking build our habits and habits are what compose our character. Until I learned this, I found out that when I tried to remember an appointment or something I needed to do, my mind was too occupied with recollection and uncertainties.

It seems to me, that for most people it is a struggle making a decision to write things down. Why do you think this is? Is it a matter of over-confidence or of some strange brand of fear? Does it imply that you are inadequate? Does it suggest you have a bad memory because you write down your schedule for today, tomorrow, this week, next week, next month and next year?

Once a person can let his pre-occupation with self-adequacy go, something amazing happens. For *one*, it becomes an unconscious habit. With no effort whatsoever, my hand reaches for my ink pen in my pocket and records new information or an adjusted schedule immediately. If I am to meet you next year on the 18th of June at 10:45 a.m. instead of the 11th of February at 3:35 p.m. at McDonald's on Bell Road, there is almost no possibility I will not be there five minutes early, and it will require no reminder to me from someone else. My calendar is my free secretary that takes almost none of my time.

Keeping a schedule and updating it daily is a powerful tool and an excellent character-training accountability exercise.

The *second* thing I noticed is the freedom this practice gives me. Instead of spending effort to recall what I need to do or where I should be and what time something is, I can spend my time while walking, sitting or driving, praying and/or thinking about issues of substance.

Keeping a schedule and updating it daily is a powerful tool and an excellent character-training accountability exercise. Still, after the multitude of times I have shared this with people, I know of very few who have picked this idea up and practice it. This habit is a life-changer, but it involves a little exercise of will and effort.

What will you do with it? Do you have the thought, as many do, that you have so few things to schedule you don't need this idea? You will never know how life-changing this is until you try it for a period of time. Not only will you be surprised and helped, but those who depend on you will get the benefit of your improvement in foresight and responsibility. Own this thought until it is as normal to you as breathing. Own it until it sets you free to live and do and become more effective than you could ever have imagined.

For some reason, it seems to be a huge leap for a person to stop trusting their own memory and form a habit of writing things down on their daily, weekly, monthly and annual schedules. It sounds difficult, but so did learning to tie your shoes at age two or your necktie or hair band at age ten. If you are willing to form such a habit, it becomes effortless. When an appointment for lunch is requested, or when you see how much time you have for an event two weeks from tomorrow, if you have your little (small enough to be convenient and not cumbersome) planner with you, it is nearly effortless.

You may have so many things to do you don't want to take time to write things down. You may have so few things to schedule that you think it is not necessary. On this point I am a little bit stubborn. Learn to schedule, not by squeezing your brain but by squeezing your ink pen.

Whatever you know to do, write it down. Sooner or later, everything will affect your business; everything will affect your family; and everything will affect everyone you know and everything you do. So what should you write down? Well, what about the one or twenty appointments you have this week? When is your 90-day risk-free trial up for your $200.00 business newsletter? Write it down in your daily planner a week in advance to either cancel it and get a full refund, or know you want to extend it for a certain period of time.

Learn to schedule, not by squeezing your brain but by squeezing your ink pen.

When is your annual doctor's appointment due? How about your semi-annual teeth cleaning appointment. If you write them down the moment you make them, months later or a year later you know exactly what to do without missing an appointment or wondering when you should call your dentist. When was that monthly appointment for the pest control company for your office and home?

Does your wife have a birthday this year? What day? What other important days are there in the lives of your family and co-workers and employees? If their names are in the right place and on the right day in your planner, it is convenient and simple to accomplish a very meaningful thing.

When does your secretary need time away for vacation? What time was that little league game for your child or grandchild? Tuesday or Friday? Which day are you available for lunch this week with a salesman or for your mentoring meeting with a Christian brother for fellowship?

Hmmm...suddenly, so many things to write down. "How did I ever live without this?!" The day you have that thought is the day you will realize how free your mind is to think about important things, and how much easier it is for your heart to pray while you work. Your mind is at liberty to function, no longer in bondage always trying to remember what you think you should do today or trying to remember if you forgot something yesterday.

When you schedule everything, it does not noticeably take extra time. It helps you focus and prioritize; and it saves time.

Get free to live! This is a little key that only you can turn. Duplicate keys are not available and the key belongs only to you.

Let me summarize a few things related to this:

1. *When you schedule everything, it does not noticeably take extra time. It helps you focus and prioritize; and it saves time.*
2. *When you have a schedule written and updated day by day, you can use your energy for other, larger thoughts, not for constantly trying to remember something or needing to apologize for being late or missing something (again).*
3. *You never need to be reminded about a commitment. People will think you are brilliant and trustworthy because you become so dependable.*
4. *You learn to estimate what you can do with your time, both business and personal. What doesn't get done today, forward to tomorrow or the next feasible day. Keep each day cleared and your mind will be clear and your energy can be focused on events, not on failures or questions about when or if you had a commitment. Instead of spending time being embarrassed for your incompetence, or explaining why you forgot something, diligently keep your schedule up to date daily.*
5. *This exercise is both a commentary on your character and a tool in helping to form it. It helps you learn to use the only thing which you truly own: your time. Go bankrupt and you can recover; let your biggest*

dream be smashed and you will find another one; but to waste a minute of time is to have it lost forever. Schedule, write things down. By such exercise you will develop a whole new way of thinking and your thinking will bring a whole new way of presenting yourself to your job, your family and your world.

Get free to live! This is a little key that only you can turn. Duplicate keys are not available and the key belongs only to you.

17. Benefits and traps of self-employment

The best of things have their limitations and the worst of things may offer some benefits. Being in business or working for another company that nurses the passion of your life is no different. Particularly, being self-employed has both its benefits and traps.

For example:

<u>Benefits</u>

- You can focus on the job you really want to do.
- Since you are the boss, if you learn well as you go along, sooner or later you will have more flexibility of schedule than you could ever have working for someone else.
- You answer primarily to yourself, although in a sense no one ever works for himself. You answer to customers, to the banks, to your family and others, yes, but you are still the person holding the steering wheel more than you might any other place.

- You can set goals that meet your needs and that of your family instead of spending a third of your life each week doing that to build a business for someone else.

- When you make a mistake you get to learn a helpful lesson that will make you even better as a person, as a believer, and as a businessman. You pay the price, but you get the benefit of lessons well learned and earned.

Traps

The amount of time required to succeed is limitless because it is unknown.

- The amount of time required to succeed is limitless because it is unknown. Just to survive, I once had no weekdays and only about three Sundays off in one year. We had four children of elementary and middle school age at the time. That affected all of us a lot.

- Even when you come home from the day, the day may come home with you. In a real sense, I was on the clock over 100 hours a week for over thirty years. Every plan, every hoped-for holiday or vacation or church conference was always subject to change, delay or cancellation. When I had enough time to take my family on a trip, I sometimes had no money. When I had enough money, my schedule was often too full to take care of even basic family and church commitments well.

Even when you come home from the day, the day may come home with you.

- Even with protective accounting schemes in place, there was never a day when I didn't realize I could be bankrupt by noon even when things were going well. One mistake by one of my workers, or one complaint by a disgruntled customer might turn into a lawsuit that would destroy us, even if the lawsuit had no basis. Even if there were no grounds for a lawsuit, the cost to win it could destroy years of faithfulness and progress. I have a friend of the highest character who was sued and he had to spend about $15,000 of his own money in the legal system to prove there was not a problem.

- The self-employed, "small business" person is always exposed to governmental changes. People committed to saving a crayfish, or trying to lessen smog, or concerned about a certain chemical or procedure or location of work, or... Countless concerns expressed in society can paralyze you and your investment in but a moment.

  For example, even though I had an excellent reputation with the Metropolitan government, with my customers and with the State licensing office(s), I was badly hurt on more than one occasion. One of my latest surprises involved a property I bought to build business condominiums. I borrowed and spent over $600,000 developing the property with all that goes in to preparing for commercial construction. I had plans engineered, drawn and building permits approved by the Metro government building department(s). The project was permitted, financed, advertised and ready for construction .

  One day, someone who was interested in my project did some research at City Hall. He discovered it had just been registered as a condemned property. Even while I was investing and working on the property and even while it was continuing to be funded by my bank and inspected by various utility companies and building inspectors, it had been declared unfit for use.

  Two weeks after my discovery of this disaster, the Water and Sewer department called me about a leak in the sewer line I had installed after dynamiting and removing about six feet of limestone rock. Their field inspections were about six months behind schedule and they had just inspected my utilities and discovered a drainage joint had slipped and needed to be repaired before the project could be signed off. True to procedure, I was given 30 days to dig up the line and repair it or the City would do it for me at a cost of thousands of dollars.

  The project had been condemned by FEMA and neither relevant agencies nor I had been informed. What happened? A federal agency had recently re-

It is through the hard things and the seemingly impossible times that we learn the most.

corded results of an air survey done by taking photographs from an airplane twelve years before that time. According to my civil engineer, the federal government had declared my recently-purchased-property now an un-useable floodway. No insurance protected me and no redeeming negotiations could be had with the City or with the federal agency.

Nevertheless, I am responsible forever for the money I borrowed to invest in that property. There was no recourse whatsoever toward any other agency of federal or local authority. I took the risk and I took the loss. If I was an employee working for a company that had this happen, I would have lost a job, a serious thing. Far more serious, as a person self-employed, I lost a business venture for which I am forever obligated.

I could relate numerous experiences like this that came from being self-employed and bearing the full brunt of things beyond my control; even though they had been carefully decided, great ideas and approved by knowledgeable authorities, financial experts and other supporters. Of course, in all fairness I must point out, that when things went well I got the full benefit, just the opposite of this painful scenario.

Faith is not based on good news or bad news. Faith is much bigger than that, and if we are in the place of peace in Christ, we can give thanks for all the things, even in the middle of a mess.

As a believer, I have learned to deal with things in a way that are perhaps quite different than I might as an angry unbeliever. I don't mean responding weakly, I mean living meekly. If you are a "Christian boss", how will you handle such surprises? Hoping you will have no such challenges is not enough. Be realistic.

Are you prepared? I don't mean you should be afraid. I mean you should be clear about your decision with the Lord, with your family and with your community. Then, even when things become too hard you will never have to second-guess your decision. It is through the hard things and the seemingly impossible times that we learn the most. Faith is not based on good news or bad news. Faith is much bigger than that, and if we are in the place of peace in Christ, we can give thanks for all the things, even in the middle of a mess.

- You have no pension or 401K plans paid for by an employer, and you pay all of your social security deduction, not just half of it. When retirement age comes, you have no guarantee of any money to live on for your remaining years. If you were able to save and invest well along the way, you may be ok, but if something did not go well, you may join the ranks of the desperate for the remainder of your life. No matter how pure your motive to care for your family and have your time free for the church or ministry activities, this is your challenge.

  Perhaps no one is more subject to "living by faith" than the one who chooses to be self-employed. You really are on your own. If the Lord is your help, you will be helped. Pray as you ought, be faithful as you should be, yet you may be surprised at the blessings and sufferings that will come your way in the midst of your highest calling while serving among the most menial duties in life.

...education is a way of thinking and learning and seeking and living.

18. Education as a lifestyle

Education is not merely something you accomplished in the past and concluded with a diploma on the wall. No, education is a way of thinking and learning and seeking and living. Properly understood and sought, it is the drive of an inward passion, a life-time of self-motivated learning when no one else may notice or care.

Readers by passion are leaders by design; but it is not just what you read or learn that counts. Rather, such a hunger, such a daily practice forms you into a certain type of thoughtful person who lives differently than most people. Without trying to do it, you think further, you think faster, you decide more clearly and you set a direction more easily than others around you. It is not just a matter of developing knowledge; it is a matter of becoming a person shaped by what he is forever learning so he may be a help to all around him. Such a person in business most likely will find a way to be superior to his competition.

Without trying to do it, you think further, you think faster, you decide more clearly and you set a direction more easily than others around you.

The man who has nothing to learn is the man who is ready to die.

As I told my sons when they were little boys, "When times are tough and jobs are short, there is still always someone who will have enough money to want something done. In the whole city there may be only that one job, so why don't you learn to live and work in such a way that you are that one person who has work to do?!". Today, each of them is a "Christian boss", and they have demonstrated very well in their personal lives and business endeavors precisely what I meant.

Personally, unless I am very ill, I read a minimum of two delightful hours a day on issues important to understanding of world events, national economics and local, social and civic conditions, and things important to my business and my family. This is in addition to whatever time I set aside for spiritual exercises in the Bible, writing and ministry applications. My schedule is so full and so busy that I cannot do less preparation if I wish to do more productive things well.

It is a mistake to assume you have learned enough and now you need to learn no more. Consider the greatest golfer or the greatest basketball player or an expert in any field. While lesser ones in their endeavor may take it easy and excuse themselves from discipline, not so the committed man. Why does Tiger Woods take golf lessons? Why did Michael Jordan listen to a coach that could not play as well as him? What about the apostle Paul who said that compared to what he ought to know he knew nearly nothing? The man who has nothing to learn is the man who is ready to die.

Today's mountain becomes tomorrow's plateau only by exercise and you need always to be ready to climb the next mountain.

From such examples, what should we learn about education? Progress is learned and earned, not granted. Today's mountain becomes tomorrow's plateau only by exercise and you need always to be ready to climb the next mountain. Learn to love this kind of mountain climbing instead of being afraid of the challenges of the unknown.

Excellence doesn't hatch out of an egg. It is grown out of a pursuing, practicing, humble, committed life. Once you think you have "arrived" you are "finished". Nothing living ever stops.

A man with a passion for perfection is always delighted to find a new way, a better way, an improved way or further confirmation that his perfection in a matter continues to pass the current, the new and the ultimate tests.

The man who stops learning is the man who is at a dead end and a downward trail. Even on a church level, it is evident this was the primary problem in Laodicea in Revelation 3. The believers were so content and proud of themselves for all their learning that they said "we have no need". Their arrogance created a passivity that made them un-useful to God in the very thing to which they were called.

On a personal level, such a lethargic viewpoint will bring disappointment to your business endeavor. You will not likely just drift into success. It takes work, and work usually is work! Work is a different kind of four-letter word. Biblical work makes the man so the man can learn *how* to work until the work is the man and the man embodies his work. Work is not just something you do, it is who you are and what you are becoming. In the process, your diligence and dependability and your excellent attitude will enable you to provide for your family, as you must do. A life that is being truly lived is a life in which education and the vibrancy of daily existence in your life's work are identical. Many jobs, especially some government jobs and some jobs for big corporations, tend to squelch liberty and creativity.

To become all you can be, is higher, liberated management or self-employment for you?

You will not likely just drift into success. It takes work, and work usually is work!

Work is not just something you do,
it is who you are
and what you are becoming.

---

19. Assorted suggestions

1. ***Make time every day to be alone with the Lord.***

Pray, spend time enjoying the Bible and opening to the Lord about what is on His heart and what is on your heart.

2. ***Read a lot.***

Read with a broad general stroke, not just your favorite topics. Become informed of things happening in politics, economics, ministries, business and finance, humanity, world events and other basic worldly exposures. These can be accomplished at least somewhat by reading one or two newspapers a day. Additionally, read world history, church history, biographies of innovators, famous people in history, leaders and viewpoints you disagree with, spiritual leaders, etc.

Above all, read the Bible, use its words as a means to pray God-thoughts, and memorize as much of it as possible. As my beloved mentor, John Crawford of The Navigators, told me forty-five years ago, "Richard, a reader is a leader". I didn't understand it then, but I understand it now.

I have learned to always consider I am wrong until proven right. This is making myself available to God and to man...to be always open to become new...and better...and more.

3. ***Learn to give and learn to receive in many different ways.***

In any crowd there are givers, takers and receivers. Keep "taking" at a minimum. Receive so you may be humble, receive so you can learn and recover in difficulties; receive so you can be blessed by others in order that you may be further strengthened to be a giver. This will deal with the pride in your heart and develop that part in you that wants to think upon what is important to God and all that God cares for, including your church life and your family. Your business will be a blessed place.

4. ***Learn to be a friend who serves without expectancy of payback in your personal life.***

5. ***Learn to be a business person where every-***

thing is fair, honest and accounted.

For the sake of your family, do business in a way where you can take care of them well and help others also along the way.

6. ***Operate your business like you would hope others would treat you.***

Step back a moment and imagine that you are an employee working for you. What would you think about your job and about your "Christian boss"?

Assume nothing but the worst and plan for the best.

7. ***Learn to consider other views, even if you are sure you know something and have experience to prove it.***

I have learned to always consider I may be wrong until proven right. This is not reverse psychology. This is not self-deprecation. This is rejecting the tentacles that pride sneaks into the mind of a "successful" person. This is making myself available to God and to man...to be always open to become new...and better...and more. Are you ready for this kind of thinking?

8. ***Remember, you are the boss, a boss who is a Christian.***

Be friendly with your customers and your workers, but never let that kindness get tangled up with who you are. In the same sense that a dad needs to be firstly a parent and not a friend, do business well and the warm affects will follow properly and in due time with the right perspective for all.

9. ***Don't assume "things will work out" in business or personal affairs.***

On the contrary, they probably *won't* just work out. You have to become such a person that learns how to walk through things in the middle of a mess. You need to learn to go "through" things, not "around" them. In business practice and in personal circumstances, it is not what you *"go through"* but what you *"get through"* that, in the end, really matters.

10. ***Learn the wisdom of the Lord's admonition to His disciples that they need to learn from those who love mammon (i.e, money).***

Money is truly a test. To be a "Christian boss" is a huge test. It may be that God can't trust too many believers with much money because they wouldn't know what to do with it. Improper views of biblical thought about man and money deceive and derail many. Whether working for someone else or for yourself, you need to deal with money.

Knowing Christ is the currency of God's economy. How we experience Christ determines who we are and how we function in His kingdom. In a parallel sense, the currency of your country in your hand is your portion of stock in your nation. The basis of civil function in any nation is its economy, and its economy is defined by money, its currency.

How you deal with money fully explains your comprehension of what it means to live as a citizen of your nation.

How you deal with money fully explains your comprehension of what it means to live as a citizen of your nation. As a Christian, we must experience Christ for God's economy. To also be a proper citizen in our country today, we must learn how to deal with money, even while we learn to be heavenly minded while serving in our world with feet that are tired and with calluses on our hands.

11. ***Learn to communicate with words from your mouth and in written documents.***

Assume nothing but the worst and plan for the best. This may sound negative but it is actually very realistic. Realizing what could happen helps you plan for what you hope will happen.

12. ***Develop a network of business associates and happy customers.***

Keep in touch informally or even formally with an annual letter or card. Although this is good business, out of this comes long term connections that may eventually produce friends who will open to you with their needs and reveal their hunger for the gospel of Christ.

13. ***Learn to be one who asks questions more than one who always thinks he has the answers.***

Even if you have an answer, there is probably more to learn. Pick up ideas and thoughts that make daily life practical so you may be able to deal with surprises and not be set back by them.

For example, even though I lock my car or truck door by mistake from time to time, I never skip a heart beat when it happens. Why? Because I always have an extra set of keys in my left pocket. When the sky suddenly opens up and pours rain when I am in a meeting or asleep in the middle of the night, I am never distracted. Why? Because I always lock the door and roll up the windows, even if I plan to be gone for only a minute. I never struggle to make such decisions day after day, wondering if it will rain or where I put my keys. For practical things like that, I made that decision one time long ago, so I never need to re-visit the issue again. The rest of my life in those kind of decisions is on "auto-pilot". How easy is that!?"

Learn to be one who asks questions more than one who always thinks he has the answers.

14. ***Even if your job involves a lot of speaking, learn to be a good listener.***

Most people talk, few people actually listen. The world is open to anyone with an ear for others and not just for himself.

15. ***Success is not magic.***

Success doesn't just happen. You need to become a person of godly character, relevant knowledge and practical wisdom. You become the person who causes a business to do well. As an ear of corn defines and expresses and explains the seed that was hidden in the soil, so you are like a seed that will reproduce and grow something that looks like what is in you. So, "put things in the soil of your heart and mind" that will look "like good corn" when it grows up.

You need to become a person of godly character, relevant knowledge and practical wisdom. You become the person who causes a business to do well.

20. The problem of success

While "fear of failure" is an understandable concept, "fear of success" seems to be more difficult to understand.

While "fear of failure" is an understandable concept, "fear of success" seems to be more difficult to understand. I have passed through this challenge and I know others who have.

Perhaps a fear of success has more than one cause. At least we should consider that it may be the result of insecurity, uncertainty, lack of education, inferior training, little experience, inability to face new situations, or fear of making a mistake because of deep-seated pride. Or perhaps it comes from a fear of not knowing what to do if success would expose you to new things and new expectations beyond your experience and comfort level; or from a character weakness, over-protective atmosphere; or from religious concepts about being so bad you don't deserve anything good to come your way, or any other number of possibilities.

What do you think about this? In any case, if you gain respect and do well in your finances, people seem to notice. Let me share a few experiences and ask what you might do with them.

1. I recall painfully my first experience of eventually being rejected for doing well while we were living in Anaheim. My wife and I and our children had reached out to our neighbors and became quickly acquainted with them. We shared a wonderful relationship and much warm communication. When I started doing well in my business, I was able to buy a little extra material and do a little extra work myself on our house and yard. The changes were noticeable and added value to the property. The changes also made our home more functional as well as attractive. People enjoyed coming to see us and we had a pleasant atmosphere at home.

From the time my work became noticeable, our neighbors became angry and distant. Before long our kindnesses were rejected and their pleasantries had turned into hateful words and actions. Jealousy seemed to rule the day and there was no way to change it. Eventually, they would not even speak to us or look at us. We have seen this kind of reaction repeatedly in many ways and in many places.

2. Because I have exercised diligently to learn to do things well and take care of what I have, many things I do seem to last a long time. For example, I still can wear clothes I owned when I met my wife, over forty years ago. They are in good condition and are now "back in style". I am quite satisfied with such things and have no need to impress anyone with the latest price tag.

Some time ago, I drove into the parking lot at H.H. Gregg to price some appliances for one of my projects. I stepped out of my truck and noticed two men sitting next to me on their truck's tailgate. One of them immediately said, "I wish I had all your money".

I was astonished and wondered what that was all about, but I knew. Many years ago, I designed features on my truck body that are extremely functional and custom. They are noticeable and desired wherever I go. My truck had nearly 200,000 miles on it, but it looked nearly new. Why? Simple maintenance year after year for about fifteen years.

Every 50,000 miles I get Casper painted and serviced and even my workers sometimes comment that I bought another new truck. It has paid for itself in service several times. Rather than buy a truck on installment every two years, I pay one off as soon as possible and keep it for another 10-15 years and use the savings for things that don't depreciate.

Because money is a great test of our character and of our heart for God, it reveals weak spots in both.

3. The Bible wisely warns us repeatedly about the perils of temptation that money can bring. (I Timothy 6:5-12). Because money is a great test of our character and of our heart for God, it reveals weak spots in both. Listen to these verses, "But they that *will* be rich fall into temptation and a snare and into many foolish and hurtful lusts, which drown men in destruction and perdition. For the *love* of money is the root of all evil, which while some coveted after, they have wandered from the faith and pierced themselves through with many sorrows."

Money is the world's orderly way to work out its system of good and evil. It is the challenge and opportunity of believers to live unto God in such a way that they bring the money out of the world and into the domain of God's kingdom where it can benefit the work and purpose of God. For us who would work diligently in management opportunities or self-employment opportunities, the temptation is to take advantage of those opportunities for selfish purposes.

If we are in poverty, we may be distracted from God because of our circumstances. If we are successful in our work, we may be distracted from God for the same reason. Poor or rich, it is a great challenge to each believer to do all things "heartily, as unto the Lord". (Colossians 3:23). While there are many examples in the Bible such as Abraham and Solomon and the rich believers mentioned in the New Testament epistles who had great wealth, there are many others such as Moses and Jeremiah and Peter who seemed to have little or nothing of material value.

Don't just wonder "what would Jesus do" as though He is dead or somewhere else. Ask Him. He is alive, "He is now" and He is in you.

I have noticed through many years and many situations that there is a strange idea in the culture of Christianity. By getting the idea of wealth and poverty all tangled up in natural concepts, it seems there is a rather prevailing, if unspoken, concept that unless you are broke you can't be spiritual. On the other hand, some preachers now claim that God's blessing will make you rich and you are not in His favor if you haven't yet experienced wealth. I submit to you that both ideas are unbiblical at their root.

Once again, I submit to you and to all of us who believe, the bottom line: learn to know Jesus, as in I John 2:27 and Colossians 3:4. Don't just wonder "what would Jesus do" as though He is dead or somewhere else. Ask Him. He is alive, "He is now" and He is in you. He is the one who can make all the different aspects of the scriptures relative and understandable. He takes the many pieces of the Bible and makes it a beautiful, tangible picture, just as you would in putting many little pieces of a puzzle together. If we are occupied in a relationship with Him, He will lead us in all of our personal, home and business affairs.

To work well,
in the biblical sense,
is to practice godly living.

A parting thought

As a "Christian Boss" who does well in business, or as one who is not so successful; or perhaps as a typical employee who is content to work a regular schedule and maintain a tight budget, the need is the same. The need is that we all have an intimate relationship with Christ and live like we actually trust Him.

(How are you doing at this? Are you enjoying Jesus daily? Do you have others with you and around you who are like-minded? Are you reaching out to them and to others for mutual strength?)

As such people who pursue God first, we can afford to live in peace and to be at rest in our circumstances, whatever they may be. As believers, may we realize the Lord has called us unto himself. He is the beginning of our calling and He is the end of our goal.

Whatever our life entails, may we live unto Christ and have the focus and benefit of our living in the church for the glory of God.

If we have little, may we endeavor to serve others with what we have, pray much, and exercise ourselves to be not overly burdensome to others.

If we have much, may we never consider "our possessions" as actually "our possessions".

With the Lord's grace, *may we give all* by living with open arms and hands to Him who gave; may we love much, pray much, die daily, and serve others freely. If we can learn to be faithful in these things, it will be a blessing to the Lord and to those around us that we have learned well both the challenge and the blessing of being a godly "Christian Boss".

If we can learn to be faithful in these things, it will be a blessing to the Lord and to those around us that we have learned well both the challenge and the blessing of being a godly "Christian Boss".

Let work become your friend and not your master. Though it oft may come by the sweat of one's brow, that sweat is but a promptive reminder that man tends to seek his way apart from God. If you can but master the worker within, rest in that treasured, friendly place, for one who lives in peace has discovered what is his work.

Additional thoughts on work and leadership

- "Management" properly understood and vigorously applied is merely a new way to spell "servant".

- Do you wish to be indispensable? Then learn to manage yourself and others so well you appear unnecessary. (Perhaps no one will know who you really are...until they try to do without you.)

- Nothing is more difficult than keeping relationships genuinely fresh. Trade "putting down" for "reaching out".

- Nothing is more encouraging to the boss than knowing that here is someone he can count on. Nothing is more encouraging to the worker than knowing the boss appreciates and rewards that.

- When a cool head takes the place of anger that is called problem solving.

- Success? It all depends on what you do with the hard things. Do you throw the stones or use them to build something?

- Let us coin the phrase "social geometry". Applied, the shortest distance between failure with oneself and success with others is the straight line of respect, integrity, and forgiveness.

- Better an eager learner than a bored expert.

- Reaction is everything. If you presume there is a problem, there probably soon will be. Your presumption will plant the seed, your attitude will fertilize it, and your tongue will grow it.

- What is your strong point? Be advised that at some time in some way it will be the entrance into your weak point. Your weak point, in turn, is the secret of advancing into strength.

- The first step to a declining atmosphere, situation, relationship, or morale is allowing oneself to take others for granted.

- Yes, I am willing to be helped by you. The question is, rather, if your tactic involves giving me a glass of cool water or of shoving dry ice down my throat. Same material, different approach.

- A person flawless in his own eyes could never manage others. Leadership is composed chiefly in one's ability to see ahead, and to leave an imitable example behind.

- Some bosses are so mean they make death look like a sunrise.

- To pay someone for their time is an insult to divine law and to human dignity: all remuneration, even an hourly wage is irreversibly tied, not to time, but to equivalent production.

- You may not judge a book by its cover, but chances are you won't even pick it up unless the cover is attractive. Can one expect less from being prepared in education, in appearance, in a trade or profession?

- No one is so little as the one who is too big to say "I'm sorry, it's my fault."

- You may hire him because of his face and clothes, but you will fire him for his deeds for that is what ultimately shows.

- It is not possible to respect someone without respecting their time.

- Leadership is an idea as much as it is a definition of a function. As such, a leader may cut the way alone. If the idea is sound, and the way definitive, followers will arise.

- A leader is best so named by others, not by himself.

- To lead is to be. In one's being there is vision, direction. Should that ring true to observers, they will spontaneously be followers whether in business, church, or home. Such a realization will decrease the tendency to expect too much from others and to instead deal with the person in the mirror.

(The previous thoughts and sayings on work and leadership are just a few of more than 250 similar thoughts taken from the book, *Thoughts on Life and Work,* by Richard A. Nelson. You may order the book on our website, at www.mstarpublishing.com).

About the Author

Richard A. Nelson was raised in a small, rural community half way between Denver and Cheyenne. By the seventh grade he had his own lawn service of thirteen yards. This was long before the time of weed-eaters and leaf-blowers. For the next five years he worked as a box-boy in Steele's Grocery, eventually being an advanced grocery checker. This was long before digital codes and automatic price rings at a check-out counter. Although the family lived in town, during those high school years he was in 4-H and had nine projects he prepared for county and state fairs, including pigs, sheep, rabbits, chickens, electrical studies. In the seventh grade, he sang The Lord's Prayer at his brother's wedding, with 800 people in attendance. He participated in state music competitions in trumpet, French horn, and as a vocal soloist, and he was the high school student apprentice band director. While these activities seemed intense, he believes they helped form in him a work ethic and a search for meaning in life and for a personal experience of knowing Christ that has impassioned him through the following years until now.

After high school he attended Trinity College in Chicago for two wonderful, life-changing years. He acquired several degrees and counseling and teaching credentials along the way. The degrees include a B.A. in Psychology at Chico State in California (CSUC) and an M.A. in Vocational Education at Long Beach State (UCLB). He is currently working towards a doctorate in "Integration of Religion and Society" at Oxford Graduate School in Dayton, Tennessee. Richard lives in Cane Ridge, Tennessee with his wife, Christine, near their four grown children and ten grandchildren. He taught school several years in junior high school and colleges in California and Tennessee. He was a General Contractor and Developer for over thirty years, owning his own business in construction, building and real estate sales.

Richard works full time in local and international ministry, writing and publishing and maintaining his family's needs as a stock investor.

He has written many books and biblical studies, and is widely published in magazines, newspapers and anthologies. He has received many academic, writing and Who's Who awards.

Publications by
Morning Star Publishing Company

Biblical Studies:

A Biblical View of Marriage
A Biblical View of Suffering
An Overview of the Bible
Eights Aspects of the Church in Ephesians
Follow Me: Lifestyle Discipleship Series Study 1: God
Follow Me: Lifestyle Discipleship Series Study 2: The Trinity of God and the Design of Man
Holiness: the Nature of God and the Nature of His People
Romans: Building Blocks of the Kingdom
The Constitution of the Kingdom of the Heavens: Matthew 5-7

Books:

A Biblical View of Work
Family
How To Be A Christian Boss
Letting Go: Cord-Cutting Principles for a Lifetime of Parenting
Lifted Thoughts About Lowly Work
The Indwelling and Outpouring of Christ as the Life-giving Spirit
The Protestant Work Ethic: Its Origin
Thoughts On Life and Work
Work Usually Is!

Books of Poetry:

Greatness, And Other Poems
Heartcry, And Other Poems
In Her Secret Garden, And Other Poems
Portraits Of Love
Threeness in Oneness, And Other Poems
Treasures of Time
Where Are You? And Other Poems

Booklets:

Four Stages of God's Purpose
The Disciples' Prayer

Pamphlets and Papers:

A Dad Who Forgave The Impossible
A Love That Hurt
A Wasted Board In A Loving Hand
And God Asked, "Where Are You?"
Biblical Eldership
Epaphroditus and the Work of Christ
Five Aspects of the Gospel in Philippians
From A Maple Tree To A Cross
How To Raise Kids (1)
How To Raise Kids (2)
How To Raise Parents
How To Stay Married
How To Work
Joseph: In Perspective with Abraham, Isaac and Jacob
Just Dying At the Thought of Getting Old
Manasseh and Ephraim
Paul and the Whole Counsel of God
Santa Claus and The Shepherd Boy
Substitutions for Christ
The Function of Gifts in the Church, Part I
The Function of Gifts in the Church, Part II
The Household of Stephanus
The Importance of Work
The Spirit as the Life in and of the Church
What is the Church?
What Prayer Is

Printed in the United States
135806LV00003B/14/P